Fostering Children's Social Competence:

The Teacher's Role

Lilian G. Katz
and Diane E. McClellan

A 1996–97 NAEYC Comprehensive Membership Benefit

National Association for the Education of Young Children
Washington, D.C.

Cover illustration: Lura Schwarz Smith

Photo credits: Marilyn Nolt x, 4, 18, 48, 50, 58, 84, 102; Jean-Claude Lejeune 11, 16, 29, 54, 58, 87; Marietta Lynch 22; Bob Ebbesen Photography 26; Cheryl A. Ertelt 31; BmPorter/Don Franklin 33; Elaine M. Ward 6, 39, 82; Verna M. Fausey 42; Dr. Vme Edom Smith 44; Eva Anthony 62; Blakely Fetridge Bundy 65; Michael Siluk 71; Gail B. Int Veldt 74; Francis Wardle 76, 92; Nancy Balaban 78; Nancy P. Alexander 94; Renaud Thomas 97

National Association for the Education of Young Children
1509 16th Street, NW
Washington, DC 20036-1426
202-232-8777 or 800-424-2460
Website: http://www.naeyc.org/naeyc

The National Association for the Education of Young Children (NAEYC) attempts through its publications program to provide a forum for discussion of major issues and ideas in our field. We hope to provoke thought and promote professional growth. The views expressed or implied are not necessarily those of the Association. NAEYC wishes to thank the authors, who donated much time and effort to develop this book as a contribution to our profession.

ISBN Catalog Number: 0-935989-82-X
NAEYC #147

Design: Jack Zibulsky; *Production:* Donna Weiss; *Copyediting:* Catherine Cauman.

Printed in the United States of America.

Contents

3. Principles of Practice for Enhancing Social Competence 49

4. Teaching Strategies for Fostering Social Competence 63

5. Strengthening Specific Components of Social Competence 85

About the Authors

Lilian G. Katz is professor of early childhood education and director of the ERIC Clearinghouse on Elementary and Early Childhood Education at the University of Illinois, Urbana-Champaign. Her scholarly interests include the project approach, the Reggio Emilia approach, mixed-age grouping, and teacher education and development. Dr. Katz is past president of NAEYC and founding editor of the *Early Childhood Research Quarterly*.

Diane E. McClellan is coordinator of the early childhood department at Governors State University in University Park, Illinois. Her research interests include the effects of same-age versus mixed-age grouping on children's social and cognitive development, and she edits the *MAGnet Newsletter on Mixed-Age Grouping in Preschool and Elementary Settings*. Dr. McClellan has taught at the primary and preschool levels and directed the Learning Tree, one of Illinois's first nonprofit child care and after-school programs.

Preface

There is little of importance in our everyday lives that does not involve interaction with others. Most of the experiences people count as meaningful and significant—family life, work, and most recreation—include or even depend on relations with others. Inasmuch as interpersonal relationships constitute major sources of gratification, companionship, and enjoyment, a person's inability to initiate and maintain relationships can cause anguish and loneliness, even in the early years.

Individuals can realize their potential only within a community. Participation in any community requires knowledge and understanding of its norms, rules, and values and mastery of the skills necessary to interact effectively within it. The learning processes involved in such mastery begin at birth and must be well under way during the early years of childhood.

Early childhood educators traditionally have given high priority to helping children develop social competence. This priority is now supported by a growing body of research. Evidence indicates that children who fail to achieve minimal social competence during the early years are at risk for developing a variety of social maladaptations that can affect them throughout life (Parker & Asher 1987). By the time these children reach adolescence and adulthood such maladaptations may show themselves as academic failure, dropping out of school, delinquency, or a variety of mental health problems (Cowen et al. 1973; Kupersmidt 1983; Parker & Asher 1987). Not all such children will have these problems later in life. What research does indicate is that helping children to overcome early social difficulties should be a high-priority goal for early education providers.

Summarizing the effects of peer relationships in childhood, Willard Hartup (1991) states that they contribute greatly to both the social and cognitive adequacy with which we function as adults:

> Indeed, the single best childhood predictor of adult adaptation is not IQ, not school grades, and not classroom behavior but rather the adequacy with which the child gets along with other children. Children who are generally disliked, who are aggressive and disruptive, who are unable to sustain close relationships with other children, and who cannot establish a place for themselves in the peer culture are seriously "at risk." (p. 1)

Based on our current understanding of the nature and significance of early social development, we agree with specialists in the study of social development that the time has come to shift educational discourse from the traditional three *R*s—reading, 'riting, and 'rithmetic—to the four *R*s, the first of which stands for *relationships*.

Specifically, research suggests that the quality of children's social competence as early as the kindergarten year accurately predicts social and academic competence in later grades (Pellegrini & Glickman 1990). Furthermore Rogoff (1990; Rogoff et al. 1993), building on the work of Vygotsky, makes a convincing case that children's cognitive development occurs mainly in the context of social relationships (see Berk and Winsler [1995] for an overview of Vygotsky's theory and ideas). Rogoff suggests that to a large extent young children are essentially "apprentices in thinking" who learn "from observing and participating with peers and more skilled members of their society" (1990, 7). Thus social competence and the willingness to interact competently with others—adults as well as peers—affect a wide range factors related to learning the basics of one's culture.

Options for teachers

The purpose of this book is to present options for early childhood teachers to consider as they make decisions concerning how best to foster the development of children's social competence. We do not attempt to present a comprehensive review of the theory and research now available on children's social development; instead, we draw on the most relevant research in the context of each topic. Our approach is to describe the many ways that teachers can help young children with their social development by addressing the common problems and situations that arise in teaching typical children between the ages of about 3 to 6 years. We also point out some common teacher practices that may undermine the development of social competence.

While our focus is on the role of teachers during the early years, many of the principles and strategies discussed are useful in helping older children and adolescents in their own efforts to overcome social difficulties.

We suggest some ways that teachers can help typical children to interact competently with their peers who have special needs; however, research on the particular issues and strategies appropriate for the social development of children with special needs requires a separate book. Paul and Simeonsson (1993) take up many of these issues in helpful ways.

In Chapter 1 we present a brief discussion of the components of social competence and the factors that influence its development. In Chapter 2 we discuss curriculum, environment, and other contextual factors related to fostering social growth in young children. Chapter 3 outlines nine general principles of practice to be taken into account in helping children achieve social competence. In Chapter 4 we suggest some general teaching strategies for helping children overcome social difficulties, and in Chapter 5 we describe ways to strengthen specific components of social competence. The appendix presents an approach to the assessment of social competence in young children.

It is useful to keep in mind that each social interaction involves unique individuals—children and adults—who bring to bear their own personal and cultural history, emotions, and dispositions. Social interactions always occur in specific situations and in distinct environments and cultural contexts. All of these factors influence a teacher's best judgment about the most appropriate actions to take.

Children vary widely in the rate at which they develop social competence, just as they vary in other areas of development. Note also that Gardner (1991) lists interpersonal competence as one of seven kinds of intelligence, and points out that the capacity to "read" other people is multidimensional and varies from one person to another. He suggests that there are children who seem to have a "natural" facility with social interaction in the same way that playing a musical instrument or participating in sports comes more easily to some children than to others.

Throughout the text we use illustrations that include statements we have heard teachers make. We also use our own observations as well as teachers' reports of their experiences to demonstrate approaches that we believe might not be in the best interests of children's social development. We offer examples of alternative ways teachers might address the same situations. However, we encourage readers to use our suggestions as *examples* rather than *prescriptions* of possible ways of approaching children. Teaching techniques are most effective when they are spontaneous and consistent with teachers' own styles and preferences.

Just as happens with other important competencies, social competence is most likely to be acquired and strengthened in an atmosphere of warmth, acceptance, respect, and deep faith in the child's capacity to grow and develop.

Acknowledgments

We wish to express our deep appreciation to the many teachers and students we have worked with and from whom we continue to learn about helping children develop the capacity for satisfying relationships with their peers.

We also want to thank the staff of the ERIC Clearinghouse on Elementary and Early Childhood Education at the University of Illinois for their constant assistance in gaining access to current research and other information resources.

Finally, we wish to thank our families for their patience and their help.

Social Competence in the Early Years

Competence in building and maintaining relationships with others involves a complex interplay of feelings, thought, and skills. While these components take a long time to learn, their foundations are laid early in childhood by responsive, patient, and supportive parents, teachers, and other adults, and in the context of a variety of opportunities to interact with peers. This chapter presents an overview of the components of social competence and influences on their development, and a discussion of common social difficulties.

Social competence defined

Although definitions of social competence vary, they generally focus on an individual's ability to initiate and maintain satisfying, reciprocal relationships with peers. Waters and Sroufe (1983) define competence in general as the "ability to generate and coordinate flexible, adaptive responses to demands and to generate and capitalize on opportunities in the environment" (p. 80). In other words, the competent individual is a person who can use environmental and personal resources to achieve a good developmental outcome—an outcome that makes possible satisfying and competent participation in and contributions to the groups, communities, and larger society to which one belongs.

Waters and Sroufe's general definition of competence suggests that socially competent young children are those who engage in satisfying interactions and activities with adults and peers and through such interactions further improve their own competence.

Popularity and friendship

Specialists in social development distinguish between two aspects of social competence: peer status or popularity (usually referred to as *sociometric status*) and friendship. Vandell and Hembree (1994) maintain that the terms *peer status* and *popularity* refer to the extent to which children are accepted or rejected by their peers. However, they state,

Friendship is distinguished from peer social status by its directionality and specificity. Whereas peer status is unilateral and measures the extent to which a child is liked or accepted by a peer group, friendship is a dyadic relationship requiring mutual selection between two specific children. (p. 462)

Thus it is possible for a child to be accepted by some peers without developing the reciprocal acceptance that characterizes friendships. That is, a child can be popular without developing any actual friendships. Conversely, a child can be unpopular and yet maintain one or more friendships. Although the capacity for friendship most likely has greater significance for long-term development than does popularity, both of these aspects of social competence warrant the concern of parents and teachers of young children.

Sociability and intimacy

Emphasis on strengthening social competence does not imply that teachers should expect all children to be social butterflies who are popular with all their classmates. The important factor in assessing a child's social development may be the quality rather than the quantity of peer relationships.

A person may be sociable and easygoing with many people yet lack the capacity to feel deeply attached to, care for, or feel responsible for a few friends and engage in intimate reciprocal give-and-take with them. It is likely that friendship, more than popularity and sociability, enhances mental health and quality of life throughout the life span. Therefore, when assessing social development, it is important to be aware of this distinction and to ascertain children's capacity to form intimate, caring, reciprocal relationships with a few peers. It is also likely, however, that a wide continuum exists in children's experience and expression of intimacy versus group affiliation, and that there is room for variation without teachers becoming alarmed or alarming the child's parents.

Socially competent young children engage in satisfying interactions and activities with adults and peers and through such interactions further improve their own competence.

The more time children spend in group settings during their early years, the more opportunity the teacher has to observe and interact with each child and his or her parents. This increased involvement as a central person in the child's life brings with it a need for teachers to be able to distinguish between healthy variations in children's styles of relating to others and variations signaling a child's need for some extra help in developing satisfying relationships with other children.

Components of social competence

Paul and Lonzel, both 5 years old, are engrossed in building a fort with Legos. James, also 5, approaches them with the desire to be included in their play. "Let's make a skyscraper!" he suggests, grabbing several Legos. Paul and Lonzel, startled, look up at James. "Go away! You can't play with us!" they state emphatically, turning away. Eyes downcast, James wanders off feeling forlorn and wondering why the others don't want to play with him.

In another part of the kindergarten room, Alissa and Jonathan are playing "restaurant." Kara quietly approaches the two children. They glance at Kara and say hi but do not invite her to join the play. Kara watches unobtrusively for a few minutes.

"Here's your hamburger and fries, ma'am," says Jonathan as he sets a plate down in front of Alissa.

"Thank you, waitress [sic]," Alissa responds.

"That looks delicious," comments Kara.

Jonathan turns to Kara and asks, "Would you like something to eat?"

"Yes, please," says Kara.

Kara's inclusion in the group successfully achieved, the three children play together for the rest of the morning.

In the cases of Kara and James, we see differences in children's social competence that involve emotion regulation, social knowledge, and social understanding as well as the social skills needed to act on that knowledge and understanding.

Children's ability to regulate their emotions is a major contributor to the development of both peer status and friendships (Denham, Renwick-Debardi, & Hewes 1994; Fox 1994). The ability to develop friendships also depends on the acquisition of many kinds of social knowledge, understanding, and interaction skills. Most social interaction involves elements of all of these components. For example, a basic competence required for successful peer-group interaction is turn taking. To take turns successfully a child must be able to postpone her wishes, understand that taking turns is expected and normal in the social context, and behave appropriately when her turn finally comes.

Emotion regulation

A major achievement of the early childhood years is the development of the ability to regulate emotions. Emotion regulation is defined as

the ability to respond to the ongoing demands of experience with the range of emotions in a manner that is socially tolerable and sufficiently flexible to permit spontaneous reactions as well as the ability to delay spontaneous reactions as needed. (Cole, Michel, & Teti 1994, 76)

Emotions form the underlying bases for motivation, provoke problem-solving, and stimulate participation in a wide variety of activities and situations. Emotions are essential adaptive capacities that contribute to survival. (p. 81)

The ability to regulate emotions—for example, to control frustration long enough to resolve a conflict—develops from interaction with primary caregivers and from the child's inborn temperament (Calkins 1994). From the caregiver's sensitive responses a child gradually learns to modify his emotions. To a large extent, children's emotion regulation patterns are well established, for better or worse, by the time they reach the preschool period.

During their early years children have to learn how to deal with frustration, enjoy others, recognize danger, cope with fear and anxiety, tolerate being alone sometimes, and develop friendships (Cole, Michel, & Teti 1994). Calkins (1994) states that emotion regulation comprises the processes and strategies used to manage emotional arousal so that "successful interpersonal functioning is possible" (p. 53). She explains,

The progression from relying on parents for regulation of arousal to being able to self-regulate is a process that begins in infancy and continues through early childhood. The caregiver's role in this process is extensive; initially, the provision of food, clothing, and physical soothing assists the infant in [emotional] state regulation; later, more complex communications and interactions with the caregiver teach the child to manage distress, control impulses, and delay gratification. (p. 53)

In some cases children underregulate emotions such as anger, fear, and frustration in ways that interfere with learning social knowledge and skills. In other cases inhibited children overregulate their emotions so that they resist interaction and thereby lose opportunities to acquire and practice basic social competencies. Part of the teacher's role in strengthening social competence is to help children channel and regulate their emotions constructively.

Social knowledge and understanding

Children need several kinds of social knowledge to be able to form friendships. Social knowledge includes knowledge of the norms and the main social customs of the groups in which one participates. It also includes sufficient mastery of the language used by peers with whom friendships are to be developed. In addition, participation in various kinds of peer-group play activities is eased when children share knowledge of stories, legends, heroes, and movie and TV program characters. Children like Kara, who have basic mastery of the language and knowl-

Children's capacity for close, caring friendships counts for more, in both the short run and the long run, than does their popularity or sociability.

Fostering Children's Social Competence

edge of the customs and social norms of their peer culture, are able to participate competently in their peers' activities.

Social understanding involves the ability to predict accurately another's reactions to the common events of peer interaction, to anticipate others' preferences, and to understand the feelings experienced by others. Children's growing capacities for communicating, carrying on a discussion, negotiating, taking turns, cooperating, initiating interaction, articulating their preferences and the reasons behind their actions, accepting compromises, and empathizing with others are all based on types of understanding, all of which play a part in effective social interaction.

Socially competent young children synchronize their behavior with others' by establishing common ground, exchanging information, and exploring similarities and differences (Gottman 1983). Such abilities enable them to resolve the normal conflicts that occur during play. Well-liked children are more able than less liked children to communicate clearly their intentions and preferences to their playmates, and they also express their feelings openly to them (Gottman 1983).

Social skills

Much of the social interaction among preschool children consists of efforts to gain access to play groups (usually referred to as *social approach skills*) and to resist other children's attempts to enter their own play groups (Corsaro 1985). In Corsaro's study, children met initial resistance 54% of the times they tried join play groups. In other words, substantial occurrences of conflict arise from attempts to gain or

Socially competent young children are able to synchronize their behavior with others by establishing common ground, exchanging information, and exploring similarities and differences.

limit access to ongoing groups. Children were observed switching activities and play partners frequently. Thus social approach skills are central to social participation and success.

The ways that children approach each other—social approach patterns learned during the preschool years—constitute essential social skills that can be observed in social interactions throughout the early grades (Dodge 1983). Kara, in the earlier example, approached her playmates for inclusion in the restaurant play and waited until she was able to determine the direction of their play. She then made an unobtrusive and relevant contribution to the unfolding drama and thus was able to enter into the ongoing interaction.

Other behaviors related to social skillfulness and peer acceptance include giving positive attention to others (for example, expressing appreciation for another's block building), requesting information from others about their activities (asking another what she is building), and contributing to ongoing discussions among peers (Gottman & Schuler 1976; Bierman & Furman 1984; Coie & Krehbiel 1984; Mize & Ladd 1990).

In addition, peer-directed aggression is a factor in determining social acceptance among peers. In an experiment involving 8-year-old boys, Dodge (1983) found that boys who engage in inappropriate, disruptive,

A young child may not yet have mastered ways of stating his feelings and desires, at least not clearly enough for effective communication with peers.

antisocial, and aggressive play behaviors tend to become unpopular, while boys who are able to establish sustained interaction with another child tend to be popular.

Teachers often define conflict situations such as squabbling over the use of a tricycle as problems of learning to share. However, such common conflict situations are better defined as *turn-taking problems*. Indeed, a great deal of social interaction throughout life requires skill in turn taking, such as the ability to participate in conversations and discussions within the family, at work, and in other social contexts.

Social dispositions

Dispositions are defined as relatively enduring habits of mind or characteristic ways of responding to experiences in various types of situations (see Katz [1995], for example). In other words, a disposition is a pattern of behavior exhibited frequently and in the absence of coercion, constituting a habit of mind that is under some conscious

Fostering Children's Social Competence

control; the dispositional behavior is intentional and is oriented to broad goals. Some examples are curiosity, humorousness, creativity, impulsivity, reflectivity, affability, quarrelsomeness, and avarice. Examples of prosocial dispositions include the tendencies to be accepting, friendly, empathetic, generous, or cooperative. Not all dispositions are desirable; the disposition to be argumentative, antagonistic, bossy, or self-absorbed can be linked to social difficulties.

Many dispositions are thought to be inborn. For example, the dispositions to learn, to be curious, and to form attachments to significant others are probably not learned but present at birth. However, many social dispositions—desirable as well as undesirable ones—are learned from experience. Dispositions are not likely to be learned from instruction. They are apt to be learned from models provided by the significant people in children's lives. Furthermore, for dispositions to become robust, children need opportunities to manifest them. Thus prosocial dispositions such as cooperativeness, responsibleness, and empathy are strengthened when children have ample opportunity to express them in real contexts.

Common social difficulties

Children in preschool and kindergarten settings display diverse social difficulties that can have a variety of underlying causes. For example, some children have not yet achieved sufficient impulse control to successfully take turns, negotiate, or bargain to resolve conflicts with peers. Some lack

the social knowledge and skills required for the give-and-take of peer interaction—skills that can only be learned from firsthand experience.

It is not unusual to find young children who have acquired a few beginning social skills but do not have enough confidence in their mastery of these skills to use them successfully in dynamic interplay with peers. Others are still so dependent on adults that they interrupt their interactions with playmates too frequently with requests for adult assistance.

Sometimes social difficulties stem from children's developing use of language. A child may not yet have mastered ways of stating her feelings and desires, at least not clearly enough for effective communication with peers. Or she may not have learned to articulate well the reasons behind her preferences and demands to win over her playmates. Some children are unable to stay on the topic being discussed by their peers long enough to participate successfully in the discussion.

Sometimes children are excluded from play because they have not yet developed the specific social skills needed for approaching peers successfully to gain entry into ongoing play. Or they may be shy and withdrawn and thus often ignored or isolated. Some behave as though they do not want to interact with their peers and therefore are not invited to join the ongoing activities.

For some children, early social difficulties are related to their inability to move beyond their peers' physical appearance. We have heard reports of children teasing and rejecting boys who are unusually small or wear glasses. Many young children avoid peers with disabilities that are related to their appearance. Occasionally children taunt others who have unusual first names. In all such cases, parents and teachers have a responsibility to help children work through the motives underlying their rejecting of others so that they can appreciate the positive qualities of those they avoid or tease—qualities beyond appearance, name, or disability.

Children who resist or reject classroom norms governing group participation do so for various reasons. Uncooperative and disruptive behaviors can be expressions of underlying emotional distress originating outside the classroom. However, in some cases, resistance to classroom procedures may stem from a child's increasing but poorly managed autonomy (Crockenberg & Litman 1990). Whatever the reason, such behavior often results in a poor reputation with peers that is hard to overcome.

Children's social difficulties may relate to the classroom environment. In some cases the classroom activities are too structured or academic for particular children, causing them to resist routines or instructional tasks or provoking them to alleviate their boredom through disruptive behavior. Sometimes the activities are not sufficiently relevant to the child's experience to arouse interest, and disruptive behavior may be the child's way of making the environment more interesting.

Occasionally the classroom ethos is either too permissive or too authoritarian for some children, causing social difficulties they may not have in other settings. Some children create social disturbances because they cannot perform the tasks set for them in the class, and some cannot attend to the tasks at hand because of their social difficulties.

Sometimes a child's social difficulties in the preschool classroom—especially in an all-day program—indicate that the child is not yet ready to spend more than a few hours a day in a group setting; the number of children with whom the child must interact may be too large for his stage of social development. However, since participation in a group child care setting is the most viable option available to many families, teachers can help minimize the stress on such children by providing comfortable places where they can withdraw from interaction for short periods as needed.

Children may lack appropriate skills simply because they do not have opportunities to learn and practice them. For example, teachers report that some families move so frequently that children's budding relationships are broken too often to allow them to master social skills or form real friendships.

Many of the pedagogical and curricular decisions teachers and caregivers make have a significant impact on children's social experiences. There are social difficulties, however, that cannot be addressed within the classroom and require the attention of specialists. Such cases are discussed in the appendix.

Shyness

Teresa, age 3, loves to paint at the easel. She spends long periods at various times of the day engaged in experimenting with color and shape. When other children approach her at such times she sometimes ignores them or turns shyly away. Teresa's teachers know that Teresa, although sometimes shy, enjoys the company of her classmates and has begun to forge several strong friend-

ships. *Teresa's choice to spend a fair amount of time in solitary play is not a source of concern to them.*

Teresa's 5-year-old classmate, David, also spends a considerable amount of time engaged in solitary play and is timid about asking other children to play. He especially likes to pretend that he is the last dinosaur on earth and wanders about the room unobtrusively pretending to chew on leaves and bury large dinosaur eggs. Even at 5 years old, David is gaining a reputation among his peers for being "weird," and they tend to avoid him. David's teachers are concerned about his behavior and lack of relationships, and they have spoken with his parents about developing a way they all can work together to overcome his difficulties.

As much as 40% of the U.S. population is shy, Zimbardo (1977) estimates. Kagan (1989) suggests that 80% of Americans have been shy at some time in their lives, and there is some evidence to suggest that shyness is an inherited tendency (Fox 1989). Indeed, shyness and wariness are appropriate responses for a young child in some situations; a degree of reserve indicates awareness of the strangeness of a situation and its participants. This is not to suggest that teachers should not help children to overcome shyness and learn to make satisfying contact with other children. However, most children spontaneously overcome early shyness, and pushing shy children too quickly or too hard may be unnecessary and even unwise.

Shyness, withdrawal, and social isolation can have developmental ramifications. What may be appropriate timidity and shyness for a 2- or 3-year-old can be a cause for concern when the child is 4 or 5. For example, a 3-

Children may lack appropriate skills simply because they do not have opportunities to learn and practice them.

year-old typically spends much time in parallel or solitary play and is often wary of unfamiliar others; however, this pattern is less appropriate for a 5-year-old. There is a significant difference in social maturity between preschoolers who play alone much of the time but are constructive in their play and preschoolers who play alone but in a manner that is escapist or negative rather than constructive (Gottman 1977). Rubin and Everett (1982) found qualitative differences in social competence in the play of preschoolers and contrasted *immature solitary play* with *mature solitary play*. David's frequent dramatic play as a dinosaur might fall into the category of immature solitary play, whereas Teresa's painting and other activities that lend themselves to solitary play—particularly at her age—can probably be considered mature solitary play.

In sum, research indicates that if children work or play alone primarily because they lack the knowledge, understanding, and skills required for satisfying interaction with other children, and particularly if they are rejected by other children, then intervention is warranted. However, intervention may not be necessary in the case of children who enjoy playing and working alone but who can interact competently with peers when it is appropriate.

Low rates of interaction

The range of normal rates of inter-action is quite wide. Studies of the as-sociation between low rates of inter-action in childhood and later mal-adjustment have been inconclusive (Morris, Soroker, & Burruss 1954; Michael, Morris, & Soroker 1957; Rob-ins 1974; Coie & Dodge 1983). In a fol-low-up study of fifth-grade children who were identified in second grade as anxious, fearful, or withdrawn, Hymel and her colleagues (1990) suggest that early social withdrawal (that is, low rates of interaction) seems to limit children's opportunities to develop adequate social skills, and this in turn leads to further withdrawal. They con-clude that "early social withdrawal or isolation . . . may indeed be a risk fac-tor in early development and should not be ignored" (p. 2019).

Other researchers disagree and ar-gue that children who seem to be ne-glected or are not actively sought out by their peers are at no greater risk for later life difficulties than are chil-dren at average levels of peer accep-tance (Parker & Asher 1987). It ap-pears that isolation and withdrawal in *mild* forms are unlikely to be re-lated to later life difficulties.

The studies discussed above are just beginning to refine our under-standing of the behavioral corre-lates of peer acceptance and social competence. While they do not tell the whole story of the causes and con-sequences of early social difficulties, they do suggest that the preschool years are an optimal period to help children who are experiencing difficul-ties with peer relationships (Rubin & Everett 1982).

Aggression

One of the most problematic so-cial difficulties that teachers must address is aggression. Schwartz, Dodge, and Coie (1993) point out that individual differences in aggressive tendencies stabilize during the el-ementary school years. They suggest further that there are at least two types of aggressive tendencies. One is called *reactive aggression* and is "conceptualized as a defensive re-sponse to a perceived provocation that is accompanied by some visible form of anger" (p. 1756). The second type is *proactive aggression,* "a more goal-directed behavior that is gener-ally *not* accompanied by overt signs of anger" but may be instrumental in its nature, used to achieve a nonso-cial outcome such as obtaining an object or position—"bullying aggres-sion in which the aim is to dominate or intimidate a peer" (p. 1756). Both types of aggression affect relation-ships with peers and often require teacher intervention.

Theories about why children exhibit inappropriate aggression fall into two general categories: the deficit theory and the excess theory. The *deficit theory* posits that children are aggressive be-cause they lack something, such as a social skill or sufficient impulse control. Some preschoolers, for ex-ample, may not know how to express

---

*T*eachers need not intervene with children who enjoy playing and working alone but can inter-act competently with peers when interaction is appropriate.

Young children may experience profound loneliness, sometimes as a result of family cir-cumstances such as moving frequently.

their needs or wants effectively and resort to aggression to achieve their objectives. If they learn more appropriate ways to be assertive, their need for aggressive approaches can substantially diminish.

According to the *excess theory*, children are aggressive because they cannot cope with their high levels of anger or aggression, and as a result their internal state pushes them to act out aggressively. By teaching them to control their excess anger or their aggressive impulses, teachers can help children reduce their habitual use of aggression. Deficit theory and excess theory are not necessarily mutually exclusive, nor are they the only possibilities.

Loneliness

Although we know that loneliness can be depressing and debilitating during adolescence and adulthood (Peplau & Perlman 1982), we don't often think of young children as experiencing periodic and sometimes chronic feelings of loneliness. Recent research, however, has found that loneliness does occur in childhood and can be reliably measured (Asher, Hymel, & Renshaw 1984; Asher & Wheeler 1985; Hyden, Tarulli, & Hymel 1988; Cassidy & Asher 1992). Researchers have not yet examined directly the experience of loneliness in children under 5 years of age, but it seems that even very young children may have some periods of loneliness.

Loneliness among children can be defined as a feeling of sadness coupled with the child's awareness or belief that she does not belong to a group, does not have a friend, or is not acceptable to peers. As children mature they develop more sophisticated ideas

Every child needs someone whose heart beats a little faster at his first smile, his first step, his first words.

about what loneliness means. So, for example, a child 4 or 5 years old may report that she feels lonely if she does not have someone to play with. An older child, however, usually recognizes that, even when one has children to play with, the feeling of having a friend or of genuine closeness to other children is sometimes absent (Cassidy & Asher 1992).

A child who experiences chronic and substantial feelings of loneliness is in emotional distress. Such loneliness may not be related to the child's personality but to his life circumstances (Bronfenbrenner 1986). For example, children who move frequently from one part of the country to another or from one school to another may experience profound loneliness. Adults often underestimate both the depth and longevity of the loneliness a child feels in such circumstances.

Teachers of young children are in a position to offer help to such children. Throughout this book we discuss various strategies and approaches to help children develop the social skills that can aid them in initiating and maintaining satisfying relationships with peers. In Chapter 2 we examine some ways in which teachers can help create the kinds of school contexts that can strengthen a child's sense of belonging.

The various social difficulties experienced by large numbers of children as they strive for competence in peer relationships need not be addressed by principles and strategies specific to each. Most of the principles, strategies, and approaches presented in the chapters that follow can be applied to a wide variety of these difficulties. Methods to strengthen specific components of social competence are discussed in Chapter 4.

Influences on the development of social competence

The development of complex peer interactive skills and the social understandings and knowledge that contribute to social competence are influenced by many factors. Among them are the nature of children's attachments to their primary caregivers within the family; the modeling, guidance, and support of parents and teachers; the opportunity to observe peers and interact with them; and children's relationships with nonfamily adults involved in their care and education and those involved in the neighborhood and community in which they spend a large proportion of their time.

The role of the family

Bronfenbrenner (1990) suggests that every child needs someone who is "crazy about him," a person who is steadfastly "in love with him," and whose heart beats a little faster at his first smile, first steps, and first words. Bronfenbrenner also emphasizes the importance of social networks in shaping parental behavior and, by extension, child behavior. Optimally, according to Bronfenbrenner, the child and the primary caregiver interact within a context that provides *both* with intimacy, love, and support. This context may be within a traditional nuclear family; however, other contexts also can provide the nurture and support needed for a good start on social competence. The extended family can be very important in the child's life (Halpern 1990). Extended family members can play a critical role, for example, in mitigating the impact of the stressful conditions often facing economically impoverished children.

The research of Baumrind (1973) and that of others who have extended her work on parenting styles suggest that children's overall competence, including social competence, benefits from *authoritative* rather than *permissive* or *authoritarian* parenting. Authoritative parenting in the preschool years, marked by a combination of high nurturance and high control as well as good communication and warmth, is associated with high confidence and social competence into the adolescent years (Steinberg, Dornbusch, & Brown 1992). Baumrind's work has contributed greatly to our awareness that nurturance alone and discipline alone are insufficient in helping children achieve general as well as social competence. Rather, a combination of nurturance and control, encouragement, demandingness, and communication provides the emotional and social context required for optimum development.

A large and in-depth longitudinal study comparing the effects of various kinds of care on the development of 2- and 3-year-olds (Clarke-Stewart, Gruber, & Fitzgerald 1994) reported that

our findings replicate well the pattern of authoritative parenting first identified by Baumrind (1967) as the key to predicting children's social competence. When parents' behavior offers a balance of warmth and control, she found, the children's behavior is characterized by a balance of independence and sociability. In this study a similar pattern was observed. More socially competent and independent children came from families in which they experienced both closeness and distance, both fondness and firmness. (p. 158)

However, conclusions about the effects of parenting style (as defined by Baumrind and others cited earlier) are frequently drawn from studies of middle-class, European American children (Chao 1994). Cultural patterns defined for a particular group are not easily transferred to others outside the group (Chao 1994).

Descriptors of parenting styles such as *authoritarian, authoritative,* and *permissive* do not necessarily predict the achievement of competence for, say, Chinese American children. Consider the reactions of Chinese teachers and parents viewing American and Japanese teaching and parenting episodes (Tobin, Wu, & Davidson 1989). The Chinese viewers considered the American and Japanese adults to be overly indulgent. The Chinese teachers were concerned that the children were being spoiled and would become willful, overly self-centered, and not capable of balancing their own short-term demands with the greater long-term societal need for self-discipline and selflessness.

On the other hand, American and Japanese teachers viewing interactions among Chinese children, parents, and teachers considered the Chinese teachers to be overly regimented and controlling. Chinese American children seem to do well in school and show other desirable developmental outcomes, even though the parenting styles characteristic of many of their families do not fit Baumrind's description of authoritativeness.

Other family conditions that appear to be helpful to the general well-being of children and their social development are substantial amounts of attention by caregivers during infancy, more than two years of separation between siblings, the availability of alternate caregivers within the household, and a close relationship with a sibling (Werner & Smith 1982).

In addition, there are many parenting characteristics (for example, disciplinary strategies) that influence children's social development. Dumas and LaFreniere (1993) compared mothers' behavior toward their own preschool children with their behavior toward other preschool children in a problem-solving task. They compared the kinds of behavior and affect characteristics of both the mothers and their children in cases of children who were identified as *socially competent, average in social competence, aggressive,* or *anxious* as mothers worked on the task with their own children and with children whose social competence was different from that of their own children.

Their findings support other research showing that mothers of socially competent children exhibited a "coherent, authoritative style of parenting, characterized by high levels of positive reciprocity and praise for positive behavior," although they showed disapproval and negative af-

---

Socially competent, independent children tend to come from families with a blend of warmth and control, a balance of closeness and distance.

---

fect as well (p. 1750). Competent children matched their mothers' behavior and affect.

An unpredicted finding was that unlike the average, the anxious, and the aggressive children in the sample, competent children tended to respond positively to their mothers' negative affect. Dumas and LaFreniere interpreted this finding as "an effective means used by the children to re-establish a regular pattern of positively toned interactions, to 'repair' their relationships with their mothers" (p. 1750).

The researchers note that mothers of anxious children exhibited the highest levels of negative behavior and affect among the four groups, though they changed totally when interacting with unfamiliar children. The anxious children performed less well than the others did on the task, supporting the "conclusion that the pattern of mother-child interactions in anxious dyads, marked by intrusive control, conflict, and aversive affect, interfered with task completion" (p. 1751).

A major implication of the Dumas and LaFreniere study is that the interactions of socially competent preschool children and their own mothers are marked by coherence, reciprocity, and contingency of the mothers' responses to their children's behavior. Dumas and LaFreniere conclude that

[First,] regardless of individual mother or child characteristics, the relationship with the primary caregiver may serve as an essential source of support or stress in social development and adaptation in the preschool years. [Second,] the results focus attention on the dynamic organization of interactions rather than on the presence or frequency of particular behaviors. . . . Contingent responsiveness (which includes positive *and* negative reciprocity) enables children and mothers to adapt positively to each other and to the ever changing demands of new social situations. (p. 1752)

Denham, Zoller, and Couchoud (1994) report that there is substantial evidence concerning the deleterious effects of frequent exposure to adult anger on children's emotional and hence social development, even when the anger is not necessarily directed at them. In the mother-child interactions they studied, negative emotional responsiveness of the mothers was a "negative predictor of boys' emotion understanding" (p. 935), though not so in the case of girls. They interpreted their findings to mean that boys may be especially vulnerable to "punitive socialization" (p. 935) and that, in general, exposure to maternal anger seems to impede the process by which children learn to interpret emotions.

In a large study of boys and girls, ages 7 to 12 years, Rudolph, Harmen, and Burge (1995) show that social experiences early in life are transformed into "generalized cognitive representations of relationships" (p. 1393). Their data support the assumption that schema representing early relationships with the mother (or primary caregiver) act as "a filter through which incoming and outgoing social information is processed" (p. 1393). Their report indicates strong behavioral continuity between family and peer functioning through the cognitive representations learned in the context of the very early mother-infant attachment and relationship experiences.

The family in the larger context

Extensive research on the relationships between the larger extrafamilial environment in which children are growing and their social competence has been conducted in Australia (Homel, Burns, & Goodnow 1987). Cochran and Davila (1992) summarize the Australian research as follows:

One especially interesting detail in the larger array of findings pertains to the relationship between the friendship networks of family and child. Where the parents reported the presence of just one dependable friend, the child was likely to report friendship with one or two children or membership in a small clique. Children whose parents reported a number of dependable friends themselves tended to describe peer contact with a number of equally liked friends. (pp. 192–93)

One of our graduate students (Boss 1996) met with a number of low-income single mothers of infants and preschoolers. She sought to deepen her understanding of what these mothers perceived as the greatest impediment to their being more effective parents. We were surprised by the reports concerning the extent of isolation experienced by many of the mothers and their children. It was not uncommon for the mothers to have had little or no contact with another adult for several weeks. Their children and infants frequently did not see children other than those in their immediate family. Many families did

Peer relationships provide a variety of contexts for children's social and intellectual development.

not have telephones, and they reported that television was the major form of contact with the outside world, as well as of company and entertainment.

Of equal note were the mothers' reactions when they entered an infant and toddler program designed to help them gain parenting skills. Most mothers spoke about the relief they felt as they became involved in the program and developed relationships with other mothers, staff, and volunteers.

Families do not exist in a vacuum. These mothers may have experienced greater-than-average isolation, but their experience is not unique and crosses socioeconomic and cultural lines. Our student observed that the connectedness felt by these parents strengthened their sense of well-being and their ability to adequately parent their children. In addition, the community that the children experienced seemed to calm them and make them more responsive to their parents.

In the next section we will briefly discuss the importance of community in providing a context that strengthens children's ability to thrive emotionally, socially, and cognitively.

The role of community

A community is a group of individuals who have a serious stake in each other's well-being and who can accomplish together that which they could not do alone. Historically, *community* has meant the overall social context in which people live out their lives. Community in this sense can no longer be taken for granted. And yet community remains central to children's social and emotional development.

Educational practices that ignore the reality of children's deep need for a sense of community are educationally unsound; they do not provide the conditions that promote immediate or long-term optimum social and cognitive development or emotional well-being (Palmer 1987). The absence of a sense of belonging to a community may have a deep effect on a child's development socially (Coleman 1990) and neurologically (Goleman 1995).

The role of peers

As we have just discussed, one of the most important influences on children's social development is experience within the family (Feldman & Wentzel 1990; Hartup & Moore 1990). In recent years, however, the important role that peers play in social development as children move out of infancy and toddlerhood has become more apparent (Parker & Asher 1987). If a child is rejected by her peers or is in some way thwarted in learning the social ropes from peers, a crucial source of social information is lost. Because young children are spending increasing amounts of time in group settings, their teachers are able to play a significant role in shaping children's experiences with peers. Chapter 4 offers strategies that teachers can use to foster and strengthen children's social competence during this formative period.

The importance of peers can be understood from parallels drawn with Suomi and Harlow's (1975) research comparing the effects that early peer deprivation and maternal deprivation have on the development of infant Rhesus monkeys. Suomi and Harlow

When the teacher focuses on the individual child rather than speaking to the whole group, she is more able to engage the child in actively thinking through the problem situation and to offer suggestions in a warm, supportive way.

found that peer deprivation had deeper and longer-lasting adverse consequences than did maternal deprivation. They concluded that most social learning in Rhesus monkeys takes place among peers. Experiments like that of Suomi and Harlow clearly cannot be conducted with human beings, but their results support our concern for the achievement of social competence early in childhood.

Freud and Dann's (1951) classic wartime study of a group of very young children who were separated early from their parents and who developed passionate attachments to each other indicates that these attachments seemed to minimize the emotional damage normally associated with their tragic situation—even that associated with the loss of parents. Throughout the early years these "motherless" children resisted the approaches of the adults who cared for them. A hypothesis suggested by Freud and Dann's experience with these children is that when young children are unable to develop adequate attachments to adults, for whatever reason, an emotional vacuum is created that may be filled by relationships with peers. This hypothesis implies that children with insufficient or weak attachments to adults are susceptible to early and intense dependence on peer acceptance and influence throughout childhood. Intense peer dependence is a cause for concern because peers are less likely than adults to be appropriate sources of guidance during the early years of children's character development.

It may also be that children who fail to establish satisfying relationships with peers, and especially those rejected because of their aggression, eventually find each other and form subgroups in which they find social and emotional support and acceptance. The members' sense of belonging in such subgroups depends on their shared hostility and resentment toward larger groups by whom they feel rejected (Dishion et al. 1991). The importance of early peer relationships is also apparent from the observation that preschool children seem to suffer significantly less stress in unfamiliar situations when another child, even an unknown child, is present than when they are alone (Schwarz 1972).

Vulnerability to problems later in life, evident in adults with a history of early social difficulties, may result from having been rejected or neglected children who had limited positive interaction with peers year after year

(Putallaz & Gottman 1981). It is also due in part to the persistence of certain patterns of interaction. In particular, behavioral traits related to aggression have been shown to be highly stable over time, difficult to change (Coie & Dodge 1983; Parker & Asher 1987), and predictive of later life difficulties in situations calling for social interaction.

Clearly, satisfying relationships with peers provide contexts for a wide variety of social and intellectual stimulation, challenges, and learning. However, the conclusion reached by Clarke-Stewart, Gruber, and Fitzgerald (1994) from their longitudinal study of children placed in various child care settings should be kept in mind:

> Mere exposure to other children is not sufficient to create a well-rounded repertoire of social skills that can be called upon in interactions with different children in different situations. The roles of adults and the physical environment for promoting children's social competence should not be underestimated. (p. 225)

It is likely that social experiences in the first five or six years of life provide the foundation on which all future relationships rest.

The role of the teacher

Although we found no experimental studies of the general effects of teachers on young children's social development, experience suggests that teachers can play a significant role in supporting social development, and this is the main focus of our book.

In the preschool and early school years, children probably do not learn social competence through direct instruction—lessons, lectures, magic circles, workbook exercises, or suggestive and sometimes exhortatory approaches. These teaching strategies are particularly questionable when they are attempted with a class as a whole. Whole-group instruction is not well suited to the way young children learn best, and it is very unlikely to be effective in reversing socially disruptive behavior, even if the behavior pattern is common to a sizable number of children in the class (Madsen et al. 1968).

What works well with young children is individualized guidance. It is generally more effective than group instruction for several reasons. First, a child is more likely to pay attention and engage in constructing a new understanding when she is directly involved in a situation. The more actively the young child participates in the construction of the new concept or understanding, the more likely she is to understand, absorb, and apply it. Second, it is easier for the teacher to offer the child suggestions in a warm and supportive context when he does so individually. Individual focus and the warmth of the interaction increase the child's capacity to hear and respond deeply to the teacher's suggestions.

The following chapters discuss the appropriate curriculum and environment for fostering social skills; outline some basic teaching principles for enhancing children's social competence; and present a number of strategies and approaches teachers can use to advance children's social development.

Creating the Context for Social Development

Just as parents influence children's social development in direct and indirect ways (Parke & Slaby 1983), so teachers also influence children's social development both directly and indirectly. Clearly parents influence their children directly through the quality of the interaction and care they provide for them. Their influence is indirect, however, in the physical, moral, and social-cognitive contexts they provide for children. This might be seen as parents' "management" role in the child's development (Parke & Slaby 1983).

Throughout this book we will look at how teachers interact with children and influence directly children's relationships with one another. However, the teacher also plays an important role in managing the context within which children's social interactions take place. For some children, changes in the larger context—the classroom—can have greater impact than do direct interventions in their behavior. Re-searchers on child care note that it is easier sometimes to change people's behavior by altering their environment than it is to change their behavior directly (Prescott & Jones 1985). Some of the problems teachers address through direct intervention—for example, by sending a child to the "thinking chair"—might be more readily resolved by introducing activities of greater interest to the children manifesting the problems.

For several years we have been gathering from teachers case studies of children whom they identify as having social difficulties. Having reviewed the more than 200 case study reports and discussed the strategies teachers employed for helping these children, we have the impression that the cases can be divided roughly into three groups: (1) children who bring serious social-emotional problems with them to school (that is, difficulties that originate outside of the school); (2) children who seemingly experience difficulties because, for a variety of reasons, they have not yet learned alternative ways of addressing the social situations at hand; and (3) children for whom, it seems to us, the activities available in the program setting are boring and who attempt through disruptive behavior to make the environment interesting.

For the third group, the curricular and interpersonal approaches and the contexts the teacher builds into the classroom are key in creating the conditions for children's positive social behavior and development. We have observed that if a teacher begins by considering how best to "set the stage" for classroom interaction, many of the behavioral difficulties of individual children disappear or at least become less urgent.

In this chapter we discuss how the teacher's attention to the classroom as a community—including the children and their families, the curriculum, and the physical environment—contributes to children's social behavior and development.

Community, the basis for social development

Historically children were raised in large extended families, working and playing alongside adults and other children. One-room schoolhouses of the nineteenth century functioned in many ways like a family in that close relationships developed and children were protected and nurtured in a single setting over a number of years (Goodlad & Anderson 1987; Katz, Evangelou, & Hartman 1990; Theilheimer 1993). Classmates worked together with a blend of cooperation and competition, and students experienced a degree of flexibility in their learning progression (Leight & Rinehart 1992). Older children were often responsible for the learning and behavior of younger ones, who in turn had ample opportunity to observe models of more mature behavior close at hand.

Community life began to change in the United States with the advent of the Industrial Revolution as men went to work in commercial or industrial environments. More recently large numbers of women are entering the workforce when their children are sometimes as young as several months old. In addition, decreasing family size and increased family mobility reduce children's opportunities to experience family and community contexts.

Sociologists agree that these circumstances have had a profound effect on how people create, experience, and sustain community (Coleman 1987). Parents no longer share a common center of community with one another and their children. In the past children's need for a sense of community and belonging, emotional and social bonding, and nurturance were met by the family, extended family, and larger community. Many children now need support from outside sources, according to current researchers and theorists. Some suggest that the schools, where children spend most of their time, may need to play a new role in the lives of children and families (Bronfenbrenner 1986, 1990; Coleman 1987).

*M*any parents do not share a common center of community with one another and their children.

Family model versus factory model of education

Many observers have suggested that since around the time of the Industrial Revolution our schools have been based on an industrial or factory model (Katz 1993). The factory model of schooling regards children as raw material to be hammered into standard shapes and interchangeable parts. Educators committed to this model emphasize the quality of the raw material, the efficiency of the production line, and the uniformity of the final product. It is interesting to note that although there have been attempts to "humanize" actual factories, there has been little official concern for humanizing our educational institutions! Furthermore, while it is doubtful that the factory model has ever been effective for education, it is particularly inappropriate for young children and unlikely to meet the future work demands for sophisticated teamwork these children will be likely to face as adults.

Katz (1993) suggests that a more appropriate model for schooling for young children is that of the family. Families are highly responsive to the unique characteristics and needs of their members and are marked by greater emotional intensity and attachment. In a family model of early childhood education, children and their families are embedded in the context of the school community. The model is consistent with the way people learn and develop, both biologically (Piaget 1970; Healy 1990) and culturally (Vygotsky 1978; Bronfenbrenner 1986).

A family/community context is not always easy to achieve but it can be done. In the following sections we consider ways that teachers can promote community in children's lives.

Building community

In seeking to build community in children's lives, teachers begin within the classroom. They also work to build community among children, parents, teachers, and within the broader school and community context.

Beginning with the classroom

One first-grade teacher told us that she knows her class is becoming a community when she sees that the children willingly and wholeheartedly support a classmate who is discouraged and they take pleasure in each others' successes without competition or jealously. She gave us the following illustration of what she feels is at the heart of a classroom that has become a community.

Jamal and the other first graders are writing their own accounts of a field trip to a new house being built across the street from their school. Jamal's efforts are labored in part because English is not his first language. After about 45 minutes the teacher calls the class together in a circle.

"Who would like to read what they have been working on?" she asks.

Cassie suggests, "How about Jamal? He hasn't read yet."

Jamal shakes his head no and stares at the floor.

"Come on, Jamal, we're all here to help you," suggests his teacher, deciding it may be time for a little push.

Cassie moves next to Jamal, and he hesitantly begins to read.

When a class becomes a community, children wholeheartedly support a classmate who is discouraged.

"He's just learning English," says a young boy to some classroom visitors, "so remember to be polite and listen carefully."

Slowly Jamal begins to read with Cassie sitting close to him. His words are halting at first, but when he realizes that he has the full attention of his classmates and no one is laughing at him, he finishes reading his short piece with greater confidence.

There is a brief hush in the classroom as the children, teacher, and visitors realize what an important moment this has been for Jamal, then they clap wildly. Jamal gives a shy but happy smile.

"Wow! Thanks, Jamal. I think our class can do anything we want if we put our minds to it. We're becoming a real family," comments the teacher.

This example shows evidence of a community climate nurtured by the teacher. It is not something that the teacher does for the children; it is something she helps the children do with and for one another. Jamal's success is not his alone; it belongs to the whole class and creates a spirit in which everyone is on the same team.

Traditional focus on the individual. When we consider our observations of the classrooms that function as communities and compare them to available research we realize that very little in the literature addresses the classroom as a community or acknowledges children's need for community. Most of the literature on children's social development is about the individual child, classroom management, the child in relationship to peers, the child's self-esteem as related to acceptance by peers, and helping the child without social skills gain them so she will be accepted by her peers. The focus is helping the individual child establish herself in the group. While this research is invaluable and we refer to it frequently in this book, we want to emphasize creating a community feeling and a supportive, cooperative classroom climate as part of the teacher's role in the development of social competence.

Increased attention to community. Those who study schools and classrooms that are particularly effective put community at the top of the list when describing what makes schools work (Wood 1992). Many schools around the country are exploring approaches to deepen children's experience of school as a community, including creating smaller schools, schools within schools, and, in the upper grades, schedules wherein children spend one period a day in a homeroom that remains the same throughout their three or four year attendance at the school. In some schools, the doors open at 7:30 A.M. or earlier and close at 5:00 P.M., depending on the needs of the children.

Deliberately setting up routines or taking time to strengthen the classroom sense of "one for all and all for one" is very important and varies according to the age of the children. Music and singing are powerful ways of experiencing being together for people of all ages. Children enjoy preparing food together (for a parent program, a class celebration, or a meal for a homeless shelter). They can dance together and perform brief plays they have written and staged. When a classmate is ill, the other children may make cards and drawings to let her know she is missed. In ways like these, children develop an increasing sense of community.

Children who are excluded: A bold experiment. Vivian Paley has observed and written extensively about children's social interactions. One issue that puzzled her, as it does many teachers of young children, was what to do about children who are left out or rejected by other children in play groups (Paley 1992). The pain experienced by children who are excluded is clear and may have long-lasting effects (Parker & Asher 1987).

Paley offers an example of how teachers may have more power than they realize to shape the conditions for social interaction within the classroom and thus change the social climate for individual children as well as the classroom as a whole. After consulting with children in her kindergarten class and children in first through fifth grade, Paley began to question whether exclusion from play groups was an inevitable part of some children's social reality. She challenged the notion that it was all right for some children to exclude others and decided to see what would happen if children were not allowed to do so. After discussing exclusion with the children in her classroom—how it felt, and whether it was really necessary—Paley moved ahead with a new classroom rule:

You can't say "You can't play."

The new rule was posted around the classroom, and children understood that excluding others in play was as much against the rules as was hitting others. Although this rule was not without controversy among the children, Paley reported that the overall social climate of the classroom improved markedly.

There are many ways to achieve community in the classroom. What worked for Paley may not work for others. However, the teacher's role in ensuring that every child feels a part of the classroom community is of major importance. It is the first and most crucial step in helping children gain social confidence and social competence. In the following section, we discuss the benefits to children when this core of community is opened to parents, the rest of the school, and the community beyond the school. The benefits flow both ways: from the school to the broader community and also back into the school, strengthening the well-being and social development of the children within the classroom.

---

*T*o gain social competence, each child must feel a part of the classroom community.

Including parents and the broader school community

In families in which both parents work outside the home, children are no longer a natural and integral part of their parents' daily routine. Parents likewise are cut off from large parts of their children's lives. Because parents and children have fewer common contexts, extra thought and effort must be given to helping parents enter their children's school context. Many teachers we work with have expressed the wish that parents had more time to be involved in their children's classrooms. Some parents, however, may feel too pressured to be active in the school, while others may believe it is the responsibility of the school to educate their children. Teachers and schools working to create a sense of community for children can reach beyond the classroom to draw in parents and the larger school community as well.

Inclusiveness. One place where we have seen the concept of community expanded beyond the classroom walls is in Reggio Emilia. This small northern Italian city is renowned for the excellence of its preprimary schools. Several things related to the overall sense of community strike visitors to the schools in Reggio Emilia. The sense of inclusiveness among children, adults, parents, and staff is one of the most impressive aspects of their approach. For example, one image we carry from these schools is that of a child in the school yard working with the janitor to rake up the leaves. Another is the kitchen pass-through that allows the cooks and children to see each other and know each other. The

Increasingly schools are looking for ways to deepen children's experience of their school or class as a community.

children help set the tables and determine the seating arrangements for their classmates.

Warm, close relationships among teachers, children, cooks, janitors, and parents are highly valued and considered central to the experiences offered to the children. The sense of community is almost palpable in the preprimary schools of Reggio Emilia; there is a sense of inclusiveness and oneness in the environment called school.

Reggio Emilia schools maintain a deep commitment to a high level of communication among everyone involved. All aspects of school life are discussed, explored, shared. The children in the preprimary schools remain with the same two teachers for the entire three years of their stay, giving teachers and parents time to build close and strong relationships. Children document their thinking and activities during school. Classroom walls and school hallways display the children's explorations, thoughts, and work through photographs, drawings, and transcripts of their discussions. These displays draw parents into the world of school by telling them how children have spent their time.

Teachers and community. Reggio Emilia schools and many of the best early childhood programs in the United States also emphasize the community that teachers form with one another. Unfortunately, in many American schools we have noted that some teachers and prospective teachers have difficulty working in groups. Others resent the time it takes to coordinate one's actions with the actions and thoughts of others. We have found that teachers who learn to work, strategize, and share deeply with others are those who find the greatest joy in their work and are able to pass on to children a deeper sense of what collaboration is about. Collaboration is not an easy process; however, teachers need each other to share insights, information, strategies, and support. They also can give one another courage to make the changes that are important to the "re-creation" of schools for young children.

We next discuss two approaches to creating community of increasing interest to practitioners in the United States and throughout the world (Veenman 1995). Like Paley's paradigm shift about rightness or wrongness in excluding others from play groups, they explore and implement alternative approaches to children's education and social development in a world that has changed dramatically, and they may bring us closer to classrooms that are families rather than factories (Katz 1993).

Sustaining community with alternative classroom structures

Although children's need for community has not changed, the societal realities that automatically included children in communities have changed. New ways of structuring classrooms are needed to give children the necessary support to grow into emotionally healthy and socially skilled adults capable of meeting the demands of the workplace, family life, and citizenship.

Bronfenbrenner (1986) notes that young children need a few primary relationships that reliably provide both intense attachment and participation in progressively more complex reciprocal activity over an extended period. The primary source for such a relationship is the child's own family. However, with the drastic decrease over the last 40 years in the time that children spend with their families (Coleman 1990), schools have become potentially an important resource for providing children with intimate, sustained experiences with adults and other children. This type of relationship is more likely to occur when children have the same caregivers or teachers over long periods of time.

Many argue that creating a sense of community is not an appropriate role for schools; however, if schools do not step into this role it is unlikely that the void will be filled by other sources. We explore next two related examples of alternative ways of structuring classroom communities: the mixed-age classroom and the class that is "looped."

Mixed-age grouping.

Jason, who is 7 years old, is working on a project with 8-year-old Brian in a classroom in a Chicago school. They are investigating the habits of the groundhog, a local animal both boys have noticed on their way to school. The boys are poring over several books about groundhogs and reading interesting passages to one another. Occasionally Jason asks Brian for help with a difficult word or phrase.

Jason is an eager and competent reader who spent last year in a first-grade classroom where he sometimes had minor discipline problems. Part of the difficulty, his teacher soon realized, was that he already knew most of what the teacher was covering on basic reading skills. However, with 30 other children in the class she did not have time to provide the additional challenges he needed.

Nurturance, leadership, cooperative work, and certain other social skills are elicited more readily in a mixed-age setting.

Creating the Context for Social Development

This year Jason is in a mixed-age classroom with children ranging in age from 5 to 8 years. Jason's discipline problems from the year before have all but disappeared.

In another part of the classroom, two girls and a boy are working on math problems using small blocks. The girls are younger than the boy. All three children have roughly the same level of mathematical understanding. As they help one another and double check each other's work, it becomes clear that the boy, Bob, is shy and socially awkward. His teacher mentions to a visitor that the threesome has been working together for several weeks and that Bob is gradually gaining social confidence and skill.

In these examples children are developing academic skills and intellectual understanding at the same time they are developing social skills. They are members of a typical mixed-age classroom in which the age range is from two to three years. Single-age grouping is generally considered the standard way of structuring a classroom, but it is certainly not the only way. Grouping children to encompass a broader age range harkens back to the one-room schoolhouse. It is a classroom structure that may have some distinct advantages for children's social as well as academic development, especially in the early years (see Katz, Evangelou, & Hartman [1990] and McClellan [1994] for reviews of research related to mixed-age grouping).

For a child like Jason, minor discipline problems, if not addressed, may mushroom and develop into a negative recursive cycle (see the discussion of recursive cycles in Chapter 3). A child who presents a discipline problem is often ostracized by his peers, thus becoming cut off from the companionship and social feedback necessary for continued social skill development (Dodge 1983). A mixed-age classroom gives Jason the social and academic challenges he needs to be fully engaged in the life of the classroom. Bob, on the other hand, needs some time to develop the courage to "practice" social skills he may have, but he lacks confidence to try out with same-age peers.

Mixed-age grouping potentially provides an enriched school community in which children have greater opportunity to give and receive nurturance and support, whether they are younger or older members of the class. Children usually stay together with the same teacher or teachers for at least two years, and there is the added dimension of an age range broader than that in the traditional classroom.

Like all skills, social skills improve with use! It is likely that children will strengthen their social skillfulness if they have opportunities to practice a wide range of social behaviors (McClellan 1994). Many important social skills are more readily elicited and therefore enacted in a mixed-age context than in same-age context (Whiting & Whiting 1975; Lamb 1978; Zahn-Waxler, Friedman, & Cummings 1983). Social skills and dispositions such as offering nurturance, exercising leadership, working cooperatively, and expressing altruism do not magically appear when a child reaches adulthood; they are dispositions and skills that must be "practiced" and experienced as satisfying and effective throughout childhood.

In addition, research suggests that fewer children experience isolation from their peers in mixed-age classrooms than in same-age classrooms (Adams 1953; Zerby 1961; McClellan & Kinsey 1997). Children who have difficulty relating to same-age peers are often better able to achieve and sustain satisfying contact with a younger or older child. Interacting with younger children is solidly supported by research as one of the most effective ways of helping children like Bob mature socially (Suomi & Harlow 1975; Furman, Rahe, & Hartup 1979. Opportunity for such interaction is uniquely available during school in the mixed-age classroom.

Bronfenbrenner (1970) argues that segregation of people by age is a central aspect of a devastating loss of community in the United States. Some years ago as researcher Howard Lane (1947) watched the neighborhood children playing in his back yard, he noted that rivalry, aggression, and a lack of compromise were often the order of the day when all the children were the same age—whether that age was 3 or 5 or 9. However, when the children playing were of varied ages, cooperation and consideration predominated.

It may be no accident, then, that evidence suggests mixed-age classrooms are more likely than same-age classrooms to support social development (as well as intellectual and academic development). When the results of 27 studies comparing the social and cognitive effects of mixed-age and

Children who have difficulty relating to same-age peers are often able to interact more easily with a younger or older child.

same-age classrooms are summarized, of the studies that showed a difference in academic achievement, 76% favored the mixed-age classrooms. In all of the studies showing a difference by age grouping, mixed-age classrooms were more likely to support social development (Pratt 1983) (see Katz, Evangelou, & Hartman [1990] for further details).

Mixing age groups alone does not ensure that the potential benefits will be realized. Much depends on the adults' readiness and ability to maximize the potential benefits (Katz, Evangelou, & Hartman 1990; McClellan 1994).

The importance of mixed-age interaction does not negate the importance of same-age interaction. Hartup (1983) and others (Goldman 1981) have pointed out that what is learned socially in mixed-age groups differs from that learned in same-age groups and that each contributes to the child's development in unique ways. Mixed-age groups usually include same-age peers with whom skills particular to same-age interaction can be used, whereas same-age groups by definition do not include mixed-age peers.

Looping. Another way of enhancing the sense of community that children experience in school, used more in Europe than in the United States, is sometimes referred to as *looping*. In looping, children and teacher stay together for several years, progressing together from one grade to the next. A teacher may start with a class of first graders, move on with them through third grade, then loop back to begin again with a new class of first graders. In the preprimary schools of Reggio Emilia, the teachers stay with the same group of children throughout their three years in the school. Where looping is practiced in the United States, the class typically stays together two or three years. In German schools, which for many years have had looping, teacher teams and children may stay together up to six years.

Formal and informal results from this approach are very positive, with dramatic increases in children's academic attainment and continued engagement with the school community (Ratzki 1988). Teachers with experience in looping identify several social advantages: a stronger sense of community among children, teachers, and parents; social and emotional continuity in peer relationships; increased depth of self-confidence; and better opportunity to overcome shyness. Looping provides more support for children who depend on school to be a major stabilizing factor in their lives, increased opportunity to help children identify and develop basic social skills, and greater collaboration and trust between parents and teachers in working out problems (Ratzki 1988).

Program considerations that support community and social development

Oden and Ramsey (1993) maintain that the curriculum philosophy or program models implemented in early childhood classrooms "can affect the range and degree of social interactions and influence every feature of children's lives in the social environment, from the use of space to the daily schedule" (p. 216). Although the cur-

> *The physical environment has significant effects on children's opportunities for cognitive and social learning.*

riculum is seen generally as the academic and intellectual content of the child's school experience, it also contributes directly and indirectly to the social context of the child's school life.

The ways teachers plan their program and arrange the environment influence children's opportunities to acquire new social knowledge and understanding as well as practice and polish their social skills. Contextual, organizational, and structural concerns that influence the social life of the classroom community include

• how the physical environment is arranged and cared for,

• the importance of the intentionality with which teachers provide and manage time for social interaction,

• the importance of play as a major context for social development, and

• the importance of meaningful group activity as children develop skills and dispositions to explore the world around them with greater intentionality.

The physical environment

A child care director once told us a story that indicates the influence that use of space can have on social interaction and the development of community. When this director accepted the position, one of the first things she did was put a coffee pot, juice, and several comfortable chairs in a little alcove outside the classroom. As families arrived in the morning and parents helped their children take off their coats, they would often sit for a few minutes in the alcove and talk to one another. The director and teachers also greeted the children, offered them a little juice, and chatted with parents. Several years later when a new director took over, no one really noticed when the alcove was converted to storage space.

One day the old director met a parent in the grocery store who was still active in the child care center. The former director asked how things were going at the program. "Oh, fine, I guess, but we never seem to talk to each other anymore," responded the parent wistfully.

It is sometimes difficult to recognize how small changes in the physical environment can make a dramatic difference in the quality and quantity of social interaction among children, parents, teachers; and yet attention to these details can increase markedly the sense of community that families and teachers experience.

Environment as teacher. American visitors to Reggio Emilia schools are often impressed by the conviction of Reggio's early childhood educators that "the environment is one of the teachers." In a similar way, Maria Montessori (1964) emphasized having a "prepared environment" because children's responses to their environment can have important effects on their intellectual, social, and spiritual development.

In a detailed study of the effects of various types of child care on young children's development, Clarke-Stewart, Gruber, and Fitzgerald (1994) found that the physical environment of a child care center or family day care home has significant effects on children's opportunities for cognitive and social learning. They summarize their findings as follows:

The final dimension of day care that was shown to be important in predicting children's development . . . was the stimulation provided by the physical environment. . . . Being in a more stimulating home environment in the daytime, with more toys and decorations and less mess and hazards, improved children's cognitive development even beyond the contributions made by parents' or caregivers' backgrounds or behavior. It also promoted children's ability to interact positively with unfamiliar peers. . . and led to less aggressive interactions among the children. (p. 240)

The environment affects children's social interactions in at least two ways—by stimulating emotional and aesthetic responses and by suggesting a range of social interactions open to children (Olds & Olds1989).

Range of activities suggested. A second way the physical environment fosters social development is through the arrangement of equipment and materials. A variety of environments is necessary to foster the full range of social skills. The physical environment influences the size of peer groups and the types of peer interactions that occur in a classroom (Oden & Ramsey 1993). Space for large group interaction and a number of areas or centers for small group interaction of three to five children are encouraged. In addition, settings in which young children spend large portions of time should provide small, enclosed, comfortable areas to which they can withdraw when they feel overwhelmed by the give-and-take typical of healthy and vigorous play in the early years.

Another play space few classrooms offer is a large motor area—perhaps because of heightened noise levels or fear that children will get hurt. Yet young children benefit from boisterous and physical interaction (Rivkin 1995). A large motor area where children can climb and tumble safely may be particularly helpful to the shy child who is at risk for being bullied by others. When children have opportunities to interact with other children in a safe but physically engaging environment, they can build confidence in their ability to handle encounters on the playground or outside of school.

Some play centers and activities are more social in nature than are others. For example, sociodramatic play, house play, doll play, and play with blocks and trucks are more likely to elicit peer interaction than is play with puzzles, paint, or clay (Smilansky & Shefatya 1990). A context that provides children with social play opportunities also promotes the advancement of children's social skills and dispositions. We encourage teachers to explore play materials, contexts, and procedures that support rich and complex social play among children while also maintaining opportunities for individual and parallel play.

Emotional and aesthetic climate. Schools in Reggio Emilia convey the importance of creating classroom space that is beautiful, personal, and welcoming—a space where children see their work reflected around them and know that their teachers value who they are and what they are exploring (Katz 1990). There is a notable absence of smiling animals and other commercial items from teachers' stores (Katz 1990). Because these environments take children seriously and make children visible to one another by displaying their work as well as pictures of them working, children feel valued. This environment stimulates a great deal of social interaction: children discuss their projects, what they were thinking when they were working on them, possible revisions in their thinking, and what they might do next.

Time

Most of us remember times in our childhood when the days seemed to stretch endlessly before us in games of pretending with friends and neighborhood children. One kindergarten teacher reminisced,

In looking back on my own childhood, I realize that life was very different than it is for today's kids. My friends and I spent long days playing outside in the sun. It was a low-income area, but there was a large meadow down the street. One summer we built a raft in the middle of this meadow—it was our secret place—and we spent all summer pretending to travel down the Mississippi, making up all kinds of stories.

Sometimes we played something else for a few days, but then we would circle back to our raft, replay the story line, add something to the raft like a food chest or a long pole, and start with a new adventure. The following summer we picked up where we left off.

I've forgotten many things from my childhood, but I remember that raft and the closeness I felt with my friends.

Slowing down: Giving children time to interact at their own pace. Bronfenbrenner (1990) notes that one of the greatest dangers to children growing up today is something rarely discussed: the hectic pace of adult life and the ways it affects children. This situation crosses socioeconomic levels and spills over into the school environment. Moreover, a hallmark of an educational context that nurtures and stimulates the development of the child's brain, particularly in the early years, is activities that allow children to feel alert yet totally relaxed and in control of their choices (Caine & Caine 1994). This condition is not unique to children, rather, it is the primary characteristic of people who become the creative leaders of their generation (Csikszentmihalyi 1990).

Today children's "downtime" is frequently spent indoors watching TV or playing computer games (Healy 1990; Rivkin 1995). Although there may be reasons for this, such as changes in parent work patterns or neighborhoods no longer safe for outdoor play, the effects on children's development must be considered.

As we have already noted, a key element in encouraging healthy social/cognitive development is time for children to socialize with one another. Piaget emphasizes the importance that peers play in the child's social and cognitive development (Kamii 1973). It is among peers that the child confronts the beliefs of those who see things differently. By hearing others' ideas and having their own ideas challenged, children begin to evaluate and reexamine them. Social interaction with peers is, in Piaget's view, a natural source of paradox or disequilibrium that stimulates the child's social and cognitive growth. If this is the case, then one could predict that children who do not experience substantial amounts of peer interaction consistently over a number of years may show deficits in social/cognitive development (Rubin 1983).

According to Piaget it is crucial for children to have many opportunities to challenge each other's thinking and learn the ropes of social interaction from one another. If adults are continually present and in control, children tend to acquiesce prematurely to adult authority. They thus may miss opportunities to develop their own social proficiency and may learn to look to adults or managers for direction. The teacher who described her childhood summers distinctly recalled the absence of adults as part of what made that time with her friends special. She and her friends were left to leisurely work out their own rules and story line.

Balancing time spent in formal and informal activity. Evidence points strongly to the need for balance between formal and informal activity in the curriculum. In particular, research suggests that early childhood programs that are excessively teacher-directed and academic in orientation yield undesirable effects (Haskins 1985; Schweinhart, Weikart, & Larner 1986). One study found that preschool children who participated in a formal academic program showed increased levels of aggression as elementary school students. Children in the control group, who attended a traditional, less formal preschool program, showed significantly less aggression in elementary school (Haskins 1985). These findings underscore the importance of providing adequate opportu-

nity for children to socialize and learn from one another in informal contexts.

There is also strong evidence that curriculum approaches may have enduring personal and societal consequences. In a longitudinal study Schweinhart, Weikart, and Larner (1986) examined the long-term effects of three preschool programs on children from low-income families (children in a fourth group—the control group—did not attend a preschool program). Although different in other respects, two of the preschool programs emphasized the development of prosocial skills and provided a relatively informal context in which opportunities for social interaction were plentiful. In the third program, which was formal, teacher directed, rapid-fire, and drill-based, acquisition of social skills was not a priority.

When youths who had attended the three programs were compared at age 15, researchers found little difference in IQ or academic achievement. However, these youths significantly exceeded members of the control group (who had no preschool experience) in IQ and academic achievement. Significant differences among the three preschool approaches were found as children grew into adolescence and adulthood. Children from the program using the direct-instruction curriculum model appeared to be less effective than were children from the other two approaches in mitigating the damaging effects of the low-income environment on their social adjustment. In terms of delinquent acts, children from the direct-instruction program were more like the children from the control group, who had had no preschool experience, engaging in twice as many delinquent acts as members of the other two groups. Children from the direct-instruction group also engaged in more drug abuse and reported poorer family relations, lower participation in sports, and lower expectations for educational attainment than did children from the programs emphasizing child-directed play.

Follow-up research with these children at age 21 has remained consistent with earlier findings at ages 15 and 18 (Barnett 1997).

Katz and Chard (1989) suggest that an optimum rather than a minimum or maximum amount of informality in the classroom be sought. A program with *maximum informality* has few routines and little adult input or guidance, and it rarely includes group projects. A program with *minimum informality* imposes many rules and rou-tines and a great deal of adult direction. In contrast to these, *optimum informality* occurs in a program when interaction among children makes a real difference in what is planned, experienced, and accomplished, and interaction is given as much attention as those activities designed for individual or large-group activity.

Providing opportunity for children to choose their own activities. A preschool teacher from California expresses this concern:

I feel sorry for children today. Parents plan every minute of their child's life: music lessons, swimming lessons, special tutors in first grade. There's little time for playing alone or free play with groups. Leisure time is almost a thing of the past.

By hearing different ideas and having their own ideas challenged, children begin to evaluate and reexamine them.

During play children are in control of what is going on, and the pace is of their own making.

Another difference among the three preschool program types in the study just discussed (Schweinhart, Weikart, & Larner 1986) involves opportunities for children to exercise control in their choice of activities. The activities of the direct-instruction group were tightly teacher controlled and directed, while the two less formal programs consistently offered children opportunities to be self-directed in their choice of activity. This suggests that children who learn that they have the capacity and opportunity to exert control over their actions early in life may be more likely to learn to accept responsibility for their actions as they mature. Theoreticians and practitioners (Dewey 1938; Montessori 1964; Katz & Chard 1989) have long maintained that there is a strong relation between children's opportunities for choice and their sense of empowerment and positive dispositions toward intellectual endeavors.

Given opportunities for choices about how to spend their time, young children often choose to play. As they reach the ages of 3 and 4 they spend more and more time playing in the company of others. Children who spend their lives rushing from home to babysitter to child care center to swimming lessons to dance lessons experience the antithesis of what children experience in play. During play children are in control of what is going on, and the pace is of their own making. There is plenty of time for discussions with playmates, ongoing revisions of story lines, and repetition of favorite story elements. The children are immersed in ongoing social processes rather than buffeted about by outside intrusions or expectations for one-shot products.

In the following section we discuss the importance of play as a context for the development of social skills, touching on the potential, as children develop, for intellectually challenging and substantive work together on projects. In group work children continue to engage with one another in ways that encourage the development of complex and sophisticated social skills in conjunction with activity that strengthens intellectual dispositions to investigate, analyze, and make and test predictions about significant aspects of their experience and environment.

Play

A 12-month-old child is sitting in the park with her father. She hands him a toy, indicates that she wants it back, then gives it to her father again. This "game" might go on for several minutes or much longer if the father is feeling relaxed and willing.

A few feet away, in a sand box, several 6-year-olds are creating a complex city in the sand, coordinating the construction of all kinds of bridges, office buildings, homes, tunnels, stores, and farms. Occasionally they disagree about the placement of a new tunnel or bridge. Usually after a brief time they find a way to move forward in construction through compromise and reasoning.

There are a number of forms and several levels of complexity in children's play activities, such as solitary play, parallel play, rough-and-tumble play, or sociodramatic play. The above examples are social in nature. Some materials, equipment, and activities elicit considerably more complex social interaction than others among children because they require the coordinated and negotiated collaboration of two or more persons in perspective taking, cooperation, and attachment to others. The second example is not only social in nature but also involves pretending. Pretend play might be thought of as "engagement in nonliteral behaviors within the context of social interaction" (Huges 1995, 186).

Of the many forms of play, pretend play requires the most social skill. In this section we will look at some reasons for the importance of interactive pretend play in children's social development as well as ways in which play promotes social/cognitive development through practice in specific social skills.

Pretend play and complex collaboration. There are few contexts wherein the potential for complex collaboration among children is greater than during pretend play. The level of social cognitive skills needed to coordinate chosen roles, objects, and agreed-upon contexts while moving the story line forward requires a great deal of shared focus among two or more children. The level of social understanding and skill required for participation in pretend play is generally much greater than that required in other play activities.

For example, consider three 5-year-old children—Kevin, Sharifa, and Carol—who are pretending to be leopards in a jungle. They start by debating who should be the mother leopard. Kevin insists that he is the most likely candidate because he is biggest. Sharifa counters with the obvious—Kevin is a boy, and mothers are girls! "No problem," says Kevin, "I'll be the daddy leopard. Pretend that the mother got lost and the daddy and babies are looking for her." Sharifa and Carol begin to adopt the roles of the leopard cubs, mewing and asking where their mother is. Kevin says, "Don't worry, babies, we'll find your mother."

This is only the beginning. As the children act out their scenario, they are also busy inventing it, casting roles, discussing the logic of each child's role and action, and revising roles and story lines again and again. Their collaboration does not take place in a vacuum, nor is it pure fantasy. There is an underpinning of rules that cannot be violated (prompting Kevin's decision to be a dad instead of a mom) and rules that the children agree to change (their agreement to use the space under a table as a leopard den) (Vygotsky 1978). These acts of pretending, in other words, require levels of complex cognitive and social skills not called for in most of the activities these three children will participate in during the rest of day. Their concentration and attention to detail is sustained and deep, yet it appears effortless.

As we mentioned earlier, children's play behavior until recently was often studied in relation to children as individuals (Berk 1994). Vygotsky's work (1978) emphasizes the social nature of learning and development with pretend play as a significant vehicle for development. Once children can pretend, they can create their own zone of proximal (near and potential) development, that area where a child can participate in an activity with the help of another person. In pretend play children's thinking seems to be

As children play they offer suggestions, build on each other's ideas, and negotiate differences—all of which requires considerable cognitive and social skill.

more fluid and flexible and more advanced than when children are tied to the real world (Berk & Winsler 1995). According to Vygotsky, "In play a child is always above his average age, above his daily behavior; in play it is as though he were a head taller than himself" (p. 102).

Play and the development of social skill. In pretend play preschool children have the greatest opportunity to practice social skills in a content area that is highly engaging yet nonthreatening. Successful social pretend play requires the use of considerable skill, as the child must integrate two or more viewpoints—his own and those of other children—in a way that is acceptable and meaningful to all and is consistent with the story line being enacted.

Researchers have found that children who engage in frequent and complete fantasy play with peers are more popular and demonstrate greater social skill (Connolly & Doyle 1983). Researchers have also found that fantasy or pretend play is more positive, sustained, and group-oriented than is nonfantasy play.

The importance of play in the early years. For young children, then, pretend play provides a significant framework for the practice and refinement of social/cognitive skills. Because of the prominence of pretend play during the early years, children with skill in this area may have greater opportunity than others to practice the cognitive and affective dimensions involved in social competence. Put in another way, pretend play can be viewed not only as a context of interest to preschooler but also as a skill in its own right. Opportunity to develop pretend-play skills may lead children to greater competence in social development, making them more attractive play partners, which leads to still greater competence, and so forth.

Because play is such a dominant feature of the preschool and early primary years, and social interaction is such a dominant feature of play, it is reasonable to assume that these years constitute a period in which a child is particularly sensitive to the development of social knowledge, understanding, and skills. If this is so, lack of opportunities for children to play during the early years may have a more deleterious effect than lack of opportunity for play at a later stage.

Group investigation

In numerous research projects and in most theories of cognitive development as well as theories of social development, social and cognitive development are treated as separate domains of functioning (Berk & Winsler 1995). As many teachers sense, however, this is a false dichotomy. Social and cognitive development are intimately embedded in one another and indivisible except as a conversational convenience. In consequence, we believe children best acquire and strengthen their social understanding and skills in the context of engaging in worthwhile activities. Edith Moorhouse (1971) illustrates the potential social benefits of helping a child find work that he or she finds meaningful. A young, retarded boy in a British Infant School bullied other children and was generally disruptive and unhappy. When goats were introduced into the school community, he took an active interest in the goats and soon became absorbed in constructing a goat house for them. In the course of the construction, he discovered he had a knack for pounding nails. He found his place in the peer culture, and his bullying subsided.

Social development is affected by the intellectual life of a classroom. A child's social competence and satisfaction cannot be viewed as isolated from the rest of her life. Bruner (1986) found that children who participated in some type of high-level intellectual activity at some time during the day increased the richness and complexity of their spontaneous play. If a child is engaged in activity that she finds meaningful and satisfying, she is less prone to be discontented in other areas of her life, including her social relationships.

Some researchers (Prawat & Nickerson 1985) suggest that when teachers focus on both social development and intellectual development in the elementary school years, the result is that children experience greater satisfaction and are less competitive and less combative than in classrooms where the focus in on one or the other aspect of development. We wish to emphasize the distinction between classroom activities oriented to academic rather than intellectual goals. While academic goals focusing on the acquisition and practice of literacy and numeracy skills have a place in the early childhood curriculum, they are not the same as intellectual goals. Intellectual goals focus on strengthening children's dispositions to investigate, explore, analyze, hypothesize, observe, and make and test predictions about significant aspects of their experience and environment.

An early childhood program can strive to achieve a balance between activities designed for individual effort and those requiring or inviting group cooperative efforts. It appears to us from our observations and work in schools that most early childhood programs overemphasize individual effort and teacher-imposed conformity at the expense of activities in which interaction, discussion, and cooperation are integral.

Learning in cooperation with others. Educational approaches that emphasize opportunities for discussion and joint problem solving are increasingly recognized as key to the continued development of intellectual and social skills as children progress through elementary school and into adolescence (Johnson et al. 1984; Johnson 1991). These approaches are supported by theorists such as

Project work in which children investigate topics of real interest to them, build and make things together, and report their work to each other provides important contexts for intellectual and social development.

Fostering Children's Social Competence

Vygotsky (Berk 1994) and current research on brain development (Healy 1990; Caine & Caine 1994). Caine and Caine argue that there are three conditions necessary for optimal brain development or learning:

• a climate of relaxed alertness,

• content that engages the whole child in rich and complex problem solving, and

• opportunity for the child to bring to the surface or represent what is experienced or learned.

In our earlier discussion we noted that these three conditions are all present when children are engaged in pretend play. Children are relaxed, alert, fully engaged in what is often the most socially and cognitively complex activity of their day, and they are continually representing and re-representing (through discussing, acting out, and revising their story lines) what they are experiencing.

In the preschool years, emphasis on individual activity is somewhat balanced by contexts in which cooperative social interaction is encouraged through pretend play opportunities. In the early elementary years, it might be argued that the balance is heavily skewed toward teacher-directed and individual work. While opportunities for pretend play are still appropriate in the early elementary years, other strategies become increasingly appropriate as well. Of particular importance are approaches that include some of the dynamics of play and the criteria that Caine and Caine (1994) suggest are key to deep and sustained learning.

The project approach. Group project work, when judged by Caine and Caine's criteria, provides a means for children to become deeply engaged in learning about the world around them. Project work in which children explore and investigate topics of real interest to them, build and make things together, and report their work to each other can provide important contexts for peer interaction, genuine cooperation, and growth in social skillfulness (Katz & Chard 1989). As children plan their investigations and discuss their findings and difficulties, the teacher encourages them to ask for and to give each other ideas and suggestions. Thus, instead of the teacher responding to each child individually during group discussions, she might say something like, "How about you two who have been working on the clay model, have you any suggestions for this group?" In this way children develop the habit of responding to each other with ideas and suggestions and with critical as well as positive feedback on their work.

In group work the teacher can encourage children to describe their ideas to each other verbally or through drawing, to challenge each other's ideas, to test out ideas, and to go back together to the drawing board if an idea doesn't pan out. The atmosphere is usually one of relaxed excitement or alertness. In the course of our extensive experience of teaching and working with teachers implementing the project approach we have frequently observed and heard reports of children who were able to engage in constructive peer cooperation for the first time in project work. In such cases children found ways to contribute to the ongoing investigations and constructions and participate in making decisions in ways not available to them when the classroom activities consisted mainly of spontaneous play or formal academic exercises.

* * *

In this chapter we suggest ways that overall social structure of the classroom can influence children's social competence. We recommend creating a sense of community in the classroom and the potential contribution of mixed-age group and looping to it. We also discuss the effects that approaches to the classroom curriculum and physical space have on the creation of a classroom community.

When children experience their classroom as a stable and deeply caring community, the effects on their social development and overall well-being cannot be overestimated.

In the chapters that follow, we continue to address many of the issues touched on in this chapter, including how teachers can foster a community that nurtures acceptance of diversity. We will look more closely, however, at the principles and techniques that can serve teachers in their efforts to support the development of social competence.

Principles of Practice for Enhancing Social Competence

I n this chapter we outline nine principles that relate to the teacher's role in promoting young children's development of social competence. The term *principle* refers to a generalization reliable enough to warrant a teacher's consideration when making teaching decisions.

These principles are based on our interpretation of current social development theories and research, our teaching experience, and our work with teachers in a variety of settings. They are not laws; rather, they are rules of thumb that are relevant to the consequences of the many choices and decisions teachers make daily.

A discussion of the teacher's role in enhancing children's social competence touches on many aspects of early childhood education in addition to direct teacher-child interaction. For example, our principles deal with issues related to what is commonly referred to as *discipline*. Discipline encompasses the many ways adults help children comply with social norms, control their antisocial impulses, avoid activities that could endanger them or their peers, and participate effectively in the larger social contexts of classroom and home.

In Chapter 4 we present specific strategies for implementing the principles.

Children's feelings deserve respect

A basic principle that should govern all early childhood work is to acknowledge and respect children's feelings as we strive to help them become competent participants in their peer group.

Three-year-old Laura calmly says goodbye to her mother and ambles out to the playground where many of her classmates are already busy playing on the swings, in the sandbox, and at other favorite outdoor activities. The teacher notices that Laura is standing on the edge of the activity looking apprehensive. Approaching her, the teacher asks, "Where would you like to play this morning?" Laura backs away without speaking and begins to look really fearful. Kneeling to face her and making her best guess about the meaning of Laura's behavior, the teacher says, "I bet you wish your mommy were here, don't you?" Laura responds with tears. The teacher then says, "It's a bit scary without Mommy, isn't it?" causing Laura to really cry! Taking Laura on her lap, the teacher makes it clear that she understands Laura's feelings and that Laura will be safe because the teacher is there to help and protect her.

As a result of this incident, Laura and the teacher began to develop a close relationship. Laura learned she could trust her teacher to understand and accept her feelings, while she was also given reassurance and protection in the new and daunting situation she faced. Had the teacher suggested to Laura that there was

In all early childhood work a basic principle is to acknowledge and respect children's feelings and, at the same time, to maintain high expectations for their positive, cooperative, and respectful behavior.

Fostering Children's Social Competence

nothing to cry about or distracted her without acknowledging her feelings, such a positive outcome would not have occurred.

The principle of acknowledging and accepting children's feelings applies to a wide variety of teacher-child interactions and classroom situations. However, there are occasions when a child might express dislike for another child or negative feelings toward a classroom activity. To respect children's feelings does not always mean allowing children to act on those feelings.

Almost all teachers have known children who are reluctant to join in group activities such as storytime, physical exercise, or dancing. To respect the child's feelings of reluctance to participate is not the same as agreeing that the feelings are justified. The teacher can be most helpful by acknowledging the child's reluctance, then either insisting that he join in, however unwillingly, or asking the child to find an alternative, nondisruptive activity.

Similarly, when a child expresses fear of an activity or dislike for a classmate, the teacher can express acceptance of the child's emotion without agreeing with it. In applying this principle the teacher acknowledges the child's feelings respectfully while indicating that she sees the situation differently. (Although the teacher wants to help create more positive or at least neutral feelings, dismissing or condemning the child's feelings is not a respectful or effective way to begin.)

While respecting children's feelings, teachers serve them best in the long term by maintaining high expectations for children's positive, coop-erative, and respectful behavior (Baumrind 1973) toward their teachers and others. This calls for teachers to draw a distinction between being sensitive to a child's feelings and indulging the child. For example, in the case of a child with a serious allergy to a particularly irresistible dessert, the adult in charge would have little difficulty in understanding and being sensitive to the child's desire to eat the dessert. Nevertheless, the adult would not indulge the child's wishes because the risks to the child are clear.

Unfortunately, few classroom situations present such a clear-cut basis for decisionmaking. To help in distinguishing between respecting children's feelings and indulging them, the teacher can clarify for herself what is and is not helpful to the child's long-term development and what is and is not negotiable among classroom routines and activities. The teacher's own conviction about the importance of an activity, the risks to a child who misses it, the effects on other children, and the effects on the classroom as a whole are likely to play a role in her ability to express respect and stand by her requirements at the same time.

Social competence is culturally defined

Teachers of young children are increasingly likely to face the challenge of a classroom of children growing up in diverse cultural groups. Because cultures define differently the appropriate patterns of interaction and feelings between adults and children and among children themselves, accurate interpretation of children's social behavior becomes one of the most important and complex aspects of the teacher's role.

Human beings seem biologically predisposed to synchronize their behavior and emotions with those of the people around them (Cairns 1986). Family, neighborhood, and community life would be very difficult to maintain in the absence of synchronization of participants' behavior. All of us are reared in a cultural context that proscribes and prescribes most aspects of social relationships, and we take for granted these unwritten rules until they are violated. It can be jarring and disconcerting when occasionally someone from a different culture does not conform to our expectations. We feel "out of sync" and therefore uncomfortable.

It is not wrong to have such feelings or to admit to them. Problems arise, however, when we believe that what feels right or normal to us is the only right way to feel. Such problems can occur when someone in a position of influence and power, such as a teacher, does not realize and acknowledge that what feels right to him is not necessarily the only way of relating to others (see also Derman-Sparks and the A.B.C. Task Force 1989).

Mary looks into her son's eyes and, smiling, speaks directly to him. Jack, who is 6 months old, responds enthusiastically with a string of sounds of his own. Mary mimics the sounds little Jack has just uttered. Mary and Jack are engaged in the "dance of conversation" even though Jack cannot yet pronounce a single word.

The telephone rings and Mary answers it. Other than looking out for Jack's safety, she focuses her full atten-

tion on her telephone conversation. When Jack begins to get restless and fretful, Mary excuses herself briefly from her conversation and turns her attention to him. She offers him a rubber cow, naming it as she does so. Jack becomes absorbed in mouthing and looking at the cow, and Mary resumes her telephone conversation.

Ramon, 7 months old, sits on his mother's lap as she talks over the day's events with Ramon's grandmother. Ramon attends first to his mother, then to his grandmother. Intermittently his mother balances Ramon on her hip as she moves about the kitchen preparing a meal. Ramon looks intently and waves his arms around whenever his mother speaks with particular animation.

Several times Ramon reaches out for a toy belonging to one of his brothers or sisters. Family members seem almost to sense what Ramon wants and respond instinctively. They carry on their activities uninterrupted, but they also remain in touch with Ramon and one another.

Both infants are learning an essential aspect of relating to others by synchronizing their behavior with that of another (Rogoff 1997). In each instance a different culture governs the particular way in which synchronization occurs.

In the first case the infant and mother are face-to-face, addressing each other directly. The ethos is linear, task focused, and dyadic—one thing at a time. Jack and his mother might typically live in a European or North American country where parents and infants tend to relate in a face-to-face position, imitate one another's facial movements, and make eye contact frequently when interacting. Most Euro-

> *Cultures prescribe what may be shared and how much, in what ways individuals may touch each other, what may and may not be said.*

pean and North American dyads are also likely to label objects of interest in the baby's environment, just as Mary does when she says "cow" while handing Jack the toy.

Interestingly, when European American caregivers are busy with something, such as preparing the evening meal or talking with a friend, they tend to give a large portion of their attention to that task or conversation. When the baby expresses a need for the caregiver's attention (through verbalizing, banging a toy, crying), the caregiver is likely to turn her full attention back to the infant until the infant is calm again.

In the second case the infant is physically and emotionally close to his mother, moving with her, hearing what she hears, and seeing what she sees. Ramon typically might be part of a family living in Central America or many other parts of the world where infants are likely to be sitting on their mothers' laps as their siblings and extended family members work and talk together (Rogoff 1997). The ethos is multidimensional, with a number of social and work-related events occurring simultaneously.

Rogoff, whose work has taken her to Guatemala many times, has become an increasingly keen observer of that culture and has documented the differences in the ways Guatemalan mothers and European American mothers

or caregivers interact with their infants. She is attuned to the sophistication with which Guatemalans teach their children social and cognitive skills. The teaching that is passed along to the younger generation is subtle (at least to the European American mind), embedded in the activity of the moment and occurring simultaneously with other relationships and activities. Thus Ramon, unlike Jack, does not usually receive his mother's full attention; however, neither does he appear to periodically feel the sense of isolation that causes Jack to "fuss" for his mother's attention.

Cultures vary concerning how much and in what ways positive and negative feelings are to be expressed in day-to-day social relations. They also vary concerning when, how, and with whom affection, anger, hostility, resistance, and other feelings are appropriate or inappropriate, and which relationships require respect and deference.

Some cultures have very different expectations and constraints for the social behavior of boys and girls. Some emphasize cooperation, competition, or obedience more than others do. Cultures also prescribe what may be shared and how much, in what ways individuals may touch each other, what may and may not be communicated directly, and so forth. Some cultural groups insist that children fight back when aggression is directed toward them; others are less clear about what is expected in that type of situation.

Researchers have noted that cultures have implicit "display rules" that prescribe when it is or is not appropriate to laugh, smile, cry, feel

Because children with limited social competence are avoided by peers and thus have little chance to improve their skills, adults need to help them break the cycle.

sorry, and so forth (Ratner & Stettner 1991). "Cultural display rules are, in effect, instructions that regulate which expressive behaviors are communicated and expected in specific circumstances and are required in the course of growing up in a particular culture" (p. 11).

Teachers of young children cannot be familiar with the norms, values, and expectations of every cultural group represented among the children in their classroom. However, a teacher's understanding of and genuine respect and appreciation for the cultural backgrounds of the children she teaches can go a long way toward helping her interpret their behavior, feelings, and needs correctly and respectfully.

Cultural diversity among children and colleagues provides teachers with an opportunity to learn from others new skills, dispositions, and perspectives. When a teacher deepens her respect for and understanding of the cultural norms and values governing social relationships that children bring to the school setting, she can also help each child feel comfortable and integrated in the classroom group and with the norms and values of the culture of the school (see especially Derman-Sparks and the A.B.C. Task Force 1989).

As Rogoff (1997) notes, in many cultures children learn social, emotional, and occupational skills in a holistic context rather than in a compartmentalized way. This integrated kind of learning, in fact, has emerged in current theory and research as conducive to children's development on all fronts—dispositional, social/emotional, occupational, and intellectual (Vygotsky 1978; Berk & Winsler 1995). Research related to social development that tracked the subjects over a long period of time (Schweinhart, Weikart, & Larner 1986) and research on optimal brain development (Healy 1990) support Rogoff's observations. Rogoff (1997) also notes that Anglo-Americans and Europeans have characteristic patterns of behavior (for example, singular focus on objects or individuals, such as Mary's interactions with Jack) that may serve people of other cultures living and working in global postindustrial societies. It is likely that teachers who understand and appreciate their own culture and the cultures of others can better help children bridge cultural differences. It is also likely that these teachers will be able to practice and facilitate a broader range of social skills than will teachers who rely solely on their own cultural background.

Social difficulties provide opportunities to teach

Early social difficulties sometimes show themselves as resistance to group activities, classroom rules, and daily routines. Because children who regularly resist classroom routines tend to become unpopular and to be avoided by their peers, these difficulties must be addressed.

While some children with social difficulties may require help beyond that which a teacher can give, it is always appropriate to begin by providing a context in which individual children can learn effective ways to handle their impulses and interact competently with their peers. "Misbehavior" can be regarded as an opportunity to teach children alternative and more effective ways of responding to the situation at hand. After all, if young children were always acquiescent and compliant, always able to control their impulses and interact competently, they would not, by definition, need the presence of knowledgeable and competent adults!

Some of the teaching approaches outlined in Chapter 5 implement this principle specifically.

Social behavior develops in recursive cycles

The long-range, persistent effects of early social difficulties may be understood as a *recursive cycle*. In a recursive cycle, individuals' patterns of social behavior tend to elicit responses from others that in turn elicit more of that behavior and ultimately strengthen it. The cycles may be either positive or negative.

For example, children who are friendly, likable, and attractive tend to elicit positive responses from others. Because they receive positive responses, they become more friendly, likable, and attractive. Thus children with positive social attributes gain more opportunities to deepen their social understanding and extend their social knowledge as well as to practice and hone their social skills and to learn new ones. This can be described as a positive cycle that feeds on itself.

Similarly, children who are unattractive, unfriendly, or difficult to approach and enjoy are likely to be avoided or rejected by others. In response such children tend to repeat the same behavior patterns, often with greater intensity, causing further avoidance and rejection, which results in even greater unattractiveness. Thus such children are increasingly avoided or rejected. Consequently their opportunities to interact with peers and to practice and improve their social skills gradually diminish. In this way a debilitating cycle is established. Such negative cycles become more resistant to change with each uninterrupted recurrence (Cairns 1986).

Young children cannot break a negative recursive cycle by themselves. Even adults who are aware of the need to modify their social responses have considerable difficulty doing so without help. Cyclic patterns become so well learned that they seem to occur automatically. Indeed, social behavior patterns are difficult to change because they are, and should be, spontaneous; they consist largely of unself-conscious patterns of interactive behavior. Constant monitoring of one's own social behavior strikes a false note, seems affected, and is difficult to maintain for more than short periods.

Evidence suggests that, once established, differences in preschoolers' social competence and peer acceptance remain well into the elementary years and beyond (Ladd 1983). Without intervention, children entering new social situations readily assume the social status and behavior they held in previous groups (Dodge 1983). This tendency is compounded by reputational biases formed by middle childhood that make it difficult for a child to break from an established reputation even when she has learned new social skills (Bierman & Furman 1984).

Based on research, it is reasonable to assume that the younger the child, the more easily parents and teachers can help him shift from a negative to a positive cycle. When assistance is delayed until the middle-childhood or adolescent years, the probability of breaking a negative cycle and overcoming the social difficulties is substantially lower. By the time children reach the age of about ten, they have so much firsthand evidence of their unlikeableness that it is hard for them to believe they could be liked. Clearly adults' roles in helping children in the early years are among their most important in children's entire lives.

Direct communication enhances adult effectiveness

A major responsibility of teachers is helping children in the transition from home to a group setting with its own norms, requirements, and routines.

For many children, the adults who educate and care for them in early childhood settings are the first important relationships outside their families. The ethos of the group is best if it is marked by authentic, direct, and straightforward communication from the adults about the norms, rules, and expectations for participation in the life of the group.

During the preschool and early primary school years children become increasingly capable of responding to direct and straightforward suggestions and directions. Indeed, attempts to cajole, trick, or distract children are usually ineffective and do not accomplish the goal of building social competence.

For example, when a preschooler is throwing sand in the sandbox, the teacher can suggest firmly and clearly the acceptable and appropriate ways to play with sand. The teacher can speak in a tone that conveys his confidence in the child's good sense. When, on the other hand, the teacher removes the child from the sandbox, saying something like, "Let's go and see what's happening in the block corner this morning!" his authority and credibility may be weakened in the eyes of the preschoolers. If positive suggestions and directions don't work, the teacher can then remove the child from the activity with a simple explanation for doing so.

As long as adults are respectful of children and protect children's rights to express their feelings, the children are unlikely to be harmed by direct, straightforward communication about what behavior is desired, required, and expected. This principle is addressed in the strategies suggested in Chapter 4.

Meaningful relationships require content

All sustained relationships must have content. That is, individuals cannot just relate to each other, they must have something to relate *about*—ideally something of importance or interest to the parties in the relationship. Attempts to help children who are disruptive and resistant to classroom rules and routines frequently can lead to teacher-child relationships in which the main content is the undesirable behavior itself or getting the upper hand in a power struggle.

The teacher can best support long-term social development among such children by fostering relationships that center on content other than the behavior to be changed. The teacher can address the undesirable behavior firmly, consistently, and straightforwardly, and then change the subject to a topic or activity of interest and value to the child. When a teacher-child relationship is primarily about the child's misbehavior, the teacher and child become locked in a power struggle.

To honor this principle it is important that the content of relationships between teachers and pupils be primarily about the intellectual goals of the program and what the children are learning, planning, and thinking, as well as their interest in each other; the content should touch only minimally on the rules and routines. The

"Misbehavior" can be regarded as an opportunity to teach children alternative and more effective ways of responding.

Teacher intervention should not be so frequent that children have few opportunities to solve their own problems.

Fostering Children's Social Competence

child's personality and behavior constitute appropriate content for a relationship between therapist and patient, not between teacher and child (Hawkins 1986).

Teachers should assess periodically the extent to which the content of their interactions with children concerns the routines and rules of behavior rather than ideas, activities, and other intellectual concerns.

Optimum teacher intervention promotes social competence

Conflict is inevitable among members of any truly participatory group of children; it should not and probably cannot be eliminated completely. The spontaneous and inevitable social problems that arise when children work and play together put the teacher in an ideal position to advance children's social development. However, while intervention in such problems is an important part of a teacher's role, more intervention is not necessarily better.

The principle of optimum intervention (as opposed to minimum or maximum intervention) in children's difficulties can be stated thus: teacher intervention should not be so frequent that children have few opportunities to solve their own problems, but it should be frequent enough to ensure that no child falls into a negative recursive cycle. Achieving the optimum level of intervention requires knowledge of each individual in a group and constant monitoring of each member's progress. Good decisions concerning when to

stand by and let the action unfold or when to intervene depend on close observation of the interactions as well as sensitivity to cultural norms and values that may influence children's interactive styles (Tobin, Wu, & Davidson 1989; Lewis 1995).

Through careful observation teachers can assess individual children's potential for resolving conflicts themselves and their ability to assert themselves, defend their rights, and engage in satisfying and constructive work and play. Through observation teachers can also learn that in the case of some children it is wise to be prepared to intervene when an interaction seems to require adult attention. Constant observational monitoring provides teachers with the information necessary to judge the current competencies of children and the extent to which teacher assistance is warranted.

Adults' expectations shape children's characters

Adults tend to define children's characters very early. For example, within families children may be characterized as "the helpful one," "the rowdy one," "the lazy one." Among children in a class, teachers may define subgroups as "the quiet ones," "the difficult ones," "the hard workers," "the class clowns." To some extent, these shorthand identifiers serve to reduce information overload. However, there is reason to believe that children tend to adjust their behavior to fit the definitions of those who are significant to them. In other words, the attributions adults make about children's characters tend to be

> *Because observing models is such a powerful way to learn, it is important for teachers to be particularly aware of their interactions with children.*

adopted by the children, becoming self-images that they, in turn, try to live up to (Miller 1995).

Here, then, is another reason unpopular children may experience repeated rejection: it is not always that they do not know how to behave in socially skilled ways, but that they expect to be disliked and that such expectations (self-attributions as well as attributions on the part of their peers) prevent them from using the skills they actually have in their repertoires (Rabiner & Coie 1989).

Rabiner and Coie (1989) reasoned that if rejected children were induced to believe they were well liked by their playmates, their behavior would become more confident and skilled; they would in turn be more accepted by their peers, and their characters would then be redefined. This hypothesis was confirmed in their observations. (The rates of acceptance by others did not change for a control group whose self-attributions were not changed.)

Even adults have difficulty breaking out of the character definitions their families assigned them long ago. We have heard many examples of adults who feel quite capable and competent among their friends and colleagues. Yet when they visit their families, not only are they treated in accordance

with the way they were defined as children (indecisive, clumsy, timid, the "baby"), but in spite of themselves they behave the way the family members expect them to, slipping unconsciously into their childhood characters. If adults cannot resist the attributions and definitions of significant others, we can see that children would have difficulty doing so. The child identified as the class clown might feel he would disappoint his classmates should he fail to amuse them as expected!

Teachers can help children by periodically examining the ways they have identified the children in their group and changing negative definitions to more positive ones.

Teachers' interactions with children model social competence

Because observing models is such a powerful way to learn, it is important for teachers to be particularly aware of their interactions with children (O'Conner 1969, 1972). For example, when helping to resolve conflicts or offering suggestions to children about their interactions, teachers can make sure they are interacting and listening rather than just lecturing.

Teachers sometimes intervene in disagreements among children. In such cases they might determine what happened prior to the conflict and what each child's goals were. Soliciting the children's reactions to suggestions (such as, "Would it help if you put up your buildings on opposite sides of the mat?") is also appropriate at times. As long as teachers' questions are genuine and not veiled commands, children can use this approach as a model for resolving their own conflicts.

Soliciting children's ideas and remaining open to the cues in their behavior help teachers make informed suggestions. Soliciting information and ideas from children models an interactive style of relating to others and seeking solutions to problems.

*   *   *

The nine principles outlined in this chapter reflect our view that teachers who work with young children can have a profound impact on children's social development—an impact that can contribute to the quality of children's lives throughout their life span.

Teaching Strategies for Fostering Social Competence

With the infinite variety of social situations that arise even in a single group of children in a single day, teachers will find basic principles, such as those articulated in Chapter 3, useful in guiding their teaching. They also may find useful a set of strategies for strengthening and enhancing children's social competence. Helpful too is awareness of common pitfalls—teacher behavior common in many classrooms but ineffective or counterproductive with respect to promoting young children's social competence. In this chapter we describe both effective strategies and teacher behaviors to avoid.

Effective strategies for enhancing social development

When teachers use these strategies, they are more effective in promoting children's social competence and maintaining a positive learning environment.

Communicating openly with parents

Teachers' openness to children, parents, and the cultures represented in their classroom influences their overall effectiveness in teaching and their ability to foster children's social development particularly. By openness we mean teachers' capacity and willingness to express honestly and nonjudgmentally their own perspectives to parents and to listen wholeheartedly and openly to the perspectives of children and parents.

Taken with permission from a teacher's journal, the following is a description of her strategy for reaching out to a parent to gain greater mutual understanding. The teacher is from a European American, middle-class background; the children in the program, from European American and African American families of low socioeconomic status. In many ways this narrative serves as an example of both how teachers and parents can learn to work together and how they can overcome initial differences in cultural and situational perspectives.

During a class open house once, I was trying to film parent-child interactions. They were few and far between, and of those I saw, many were punitive. Given the stresses of many of the mothers with whom we work, I was not surprised. But it made me wonder what it must be like for a child to go from a restrictive home environment (many out of a very practical necessity) to one that is open and understanding.

I remember one child in particular who was 2 ½ when he came to us. Although he took to much of our environment immediately, he had an aggressive and detached attitude. As a result he hadn't formed any strong attachments to his classroom teachers before it was time for his mother to end the phase-in process (a gradual separation process that lasts a minimum of two weeks and is designed to build trust among teachers, parents, and children). Furthermore, we felt that we had established very little trust or communication with the mother.

This child rarely spent time in any one activity and had a tendency to take toys from other children as well as to push and hit. Soon after the phase-in process ended, he began to kick, spit, and bite. . . . I decided to talk with his mother. Because her own school experience had been filled with negative interactions, however, she was very reluctant to meet at first. But after finding a way to convince her that this was not the equivalent of being called into the principal's office, she agreed to meet.

At our meeting she immediately started talking about how much her son had changed in the short time he had been at the center. She spoke of his expanded verbal abilities, his in-

sistence on helping her do everything from cooking to making the bed, and his constant demands to be read to. For her, these changes were both positive and negative. Her time was already limited, and she found that his new abilities and demands put even more pressure on her than she had had before. . . . This led into a lengthy discussion about the fact that the changes she saw reflected skills and values that we promote in our program.

We spoke of our differences in expectations and our approaches to child rearing. For example, there was more emphasis on the use of language or words to express feelings and desires at school than there was at home, where actions themselves often sufficed.

Within a couple of weeks we noticed significant changes in the child's behavior, in the mother's interactions with both her son and his classmates, and within the classroom itself. For example, in the month following our meeting, the child's verbal fluency increased greatly. He also changed from never wanting to have someone read to him to frequently wanting to be read to. He stopped roaming aimlessly around the center and began finding things he particularly liked to do. He also stopped biting and kicking other children.

His mother started coming in early to have breakfast in the classroom with her son before going to work. She talked to him more and more and sometimes read him a book before leaving. She became more deliberate and affectionate when saying good-bye to him. When she did not approve of her son's behavior, she turned to teachers to see how they would handle the situation rather than giving him a quick slap.

Effective teachers are open to parents, expressing their own perspectives honestly and listening wholeheartedly and openly to parents' perspectives.

As a teacher, I developed a better sense of what he was used to at home and how to bridge the lack of continuity between the two important settings in his life. I started picking him up more and became more comfortable using physical restraint when necessary. I was more willing to set limits and be authoritative with him. I also became more direct and structured in my communication with all the children. I simplified many things.

If we had not gone beyond the classroom to address the problem, it could very well still exist. When differences between home and school, for whatever reasons, are so large, they can have a considerable impact on a child's developing social competence. Confusion can lead to fear, and fear can lead to aggression. It took much compromise on the parts of both the mother and me to make it work. And as time passed we were able to ease up on our compromises. But it changed my program and me as a teacher in ways I never thought possible, and it did the same for the child and his mother.

The teacher is delighted with the changes in the child, but equally important is her recognition that she too changed. Indeed, each party is likely to change when genuine communication occurs. Although not always easy, finding ways to deepen communication and understanding with a child's parents can be very helpful in a teacher's efforts to enhance the child's social development. In addition, it often provides the teacher with an opportunity to deepen her understanding of her own role and to gain new skills, dispositions, and perspectives.

In this era of increasing cultural diversity, open give-and-take between teachers and parents is important, especially when the cultural background of the child and family is different from that of the majority culture. A variety of strategies can help teachers not only to gain an appreciation and intellectual understanding of the cultural backgrounds of their students but, more important, to experience and take into account the children's cultural patterns.

Asking parents or older siblings to help in the classroom is one way. Taking a walk in the school neighborhood with parents and children can yield a variety of benefits to the teacher. Visits to community churches and other religious institutions when possible, attending community festivals, becoming acquainted with the art forms (literature, dance, music, and the visual arts) of those cultures represented in the classroom can also strengthen appreciation of children's backgrounds. And, of course, attending carefully to the children's verbal and body language is always helpful.

Although these activities and processes involve great effort and may seem overwhelming at first, teachers tell us that the understanding, insight, and appreciation derived from them are invaluable on a personal level and contribute substantially to their effectiveness in helping children of all cultural backgrounds.

Expressing respect for children's feelings

To avoid development of the proverbial power struggles between adults and children, teachers can express respect for children's feelings while making clear in a straightforward and matter-of-fact manner what is expected and desired.

When teachers acknowledge and respect children's feelings, they are helping to protect children's sense of autonomy, thus minimizing the likelihood that children will dig in their heels, translating any initial reluctance to comply with classroom norms into stubborn resistance in order to preserve their integrity.

We observed the use of appropriate and inappropriate strategies in the case of a 4-year-old who persistently refused to speak in the preschool setting, although her parents described her verbal behavior outside the school setting as entirely normal. (Systematic observation of the child's behavior and experiences in the group revealed that none of her peers spoke to her—we learn early to speak only to those who respond to us!)

Over a period of months, teachers tried to modify the child's behavior by insisting that she could not have her juice and crackers unless she verbalized her request, which she consistently refused to do. Finally, after much discussion, the teachers adopted the strategy of saying to the child, in a calm and accepting manner, something like, "Maybe you don't feel like talking right now. That's OK. You don't have to if you don't want to. But when you feel like it, let me know; I'll be glad to listen."

Through this strategy the teachers communicated calmly to the child that they respected her feelings and supported her autonomy. She received her juice and crackers from respectful and accepting teachers without speaking a word; however, within a week, relieved of teacher pressure, she overcame her reservations about speaking and entered the verbal give-and-take of the classroom group easily, almost in spite of herself!

Establishing authority and credibility

An adult's credibility is based on the extent to which children perceive that adult as someone who means what he or she says. The credibility of a teacher is enhanced when he stands behind his statements and follows through with quiet authority on those suggestions or directions that he feels are in the best interest of an individual or the group. A teacher can express genuine empathy toward and understanding of a child's desires without yielding to those desires if they are not in the child's best interest, as we discussed in Chapter 3.

Helping young children acquire impulse control, for example, depends in some measure on how credible the teacher's suggestions, requests, and demands are, and on whether the signals he gives concerning his expectations and standards for behavior are reasonably clear and not mixed, confusing, or ambiguous.

Authority and credibility are strengthened when a teacher expresses expectations simply and directly. They are undermined when a teacher makes such statements as "We don't throw sand," especially when the child has

Authority and credibility are strengthened when a teacher expresses expectations simply and directly.

just done so! The teacher may be trying to convey information about the norms he wants the children to learn; however, during the preschool years especially, invoking a norm is unlikely to be as effective as straightforward statements about the specific incident.

In the case of sand throwing, it is preferable to say directly to the child, "Please don't throw sand; it's annoying when it gets in the eyes" or "Sand is not to be thrown; it is to be used with the spade and containers." Furthermore, a firm statement such as "I don't want you to do that" often will suffice when the child is aware already of the reasons for the prohibition. Like adults, young children often do things they "know better" than to do!

When a teacher says, "Jason, can we sit down now?" she is sending the child a mixed message. On the one hand the child usually knows that the message is "Jason, please sit down!" On the other hand, by couching the directive in a question, she is telling the child that he has a choice about whether or not to sit down. However, the teacher is not really offering a choice, as many children realize, and the authenticity and credibility of the message (and therefore of the teacher) is strained. We suggest that the teacher is more credible when she states simply, clearly, and politely the behavior she wants.

Furthermore, double messages in such questions as "Can we sit down now?" are often embedded in a particular cultural context. As long as the child and the teacher share the same cultural background, the child is likely to understand the implicit "rule" governing the interaction: he is expected to sit down. However, classrooms often include children of diverse backgrounds, and double messages of this kind may be unnecessarily confusing.

Referring to the confusion created for many African American children, Delpit (1988) notes that indirect teacher communication can be particularly confusing to children who are accustomed to more direct assertions of adult authority and expectations. We suggest that indirect communication can be confusing to children from a number of different cultural backgrounds or from low socioeconomic status and that direct communication is appropriate for all children.

Similarly, insisting that children apologize for offending others when they do not feel apologetic can undermine the authenticity of the classroom climate. More to the point, a teacher might say, "When you feel sorry, I hope you will say so" or "I hope you will feel sorry about what happened, and that you will tell Sam that you are sorry." Even adults sometimes need a cooling-off period before they can offer an apology!

Redefining children's characters in positive terms

Teachers often tell their colleagues about children who are particularly difficult, thus spreading children's low reputations. As a result, other teachers naturally develop characterizations of

the children to fit their reputations, focusing on the children's difficulties and weaknesses rather than their strengths and competencies. This occurs even for children whose behavior is not particularly difficult. Because of the danger of a character definition (sometimes referred to as *an attribution of traits and dispositions* [Miller 1995]) becoming a self-fulfilling prophecy, a teacher can help break a negative recursive cycle by resisting the tendency to reinforce the negative definition of the child.

A strategy that both of us and many of our students have found helpful is to imagine what the child would be like without the difficulties that are causing his problems and then to respond to the child as we imagine him. In this way we can create in our minds a different prophecy for that child to fulfill. This strategy can be quite powerful in helping young children overcome negative reputations.

For example, some time ago we observed 5-year-old Ricky over a period of several weeks. Ricky seemed unable to sit and concentrate on any activity and was continually agitated and unhappy. Teacher and children alike tended to steel themselves for negative interaction whenever Ricky approached. After unsuccessfully trying several ways to change Ricky's distracting behavior, his teacher decided to try imagining him without those irritating behaviors that so often undermined his relationships with others.

Alone, away from the classroom, the teacher thought carefully about Ricky and created as full a picture as she could of how he would behave, what he would say, how he would move, interact, and talk if he were free of the impulses and habits that seemed to repel others. Several times a day she closed her eyes for a few seconds and saw herself interacting with the imagined Ricky, a calm, competent, and accessible child.

In the classroom the teacher gradually became aware of Ricky's feeble attempts to interact competently and realized that she was beginning to see more clearly the positive aspects of this child when she was engaged with him. After several weeks she and others began to see changes in Ricky. While he did not completely change his former behavior patterns, he did become a calmer, better grounded, and happier child.

This approach can be effective because the teacher's new definition of the child's character helps her become aware of the child's positive behaviors, which she may have overlooked. A negative definition of a child's character can cause the teacher to focus almost exclusively on problematic behaviors and be constantly alert for them, thus failing to notice the child's weak and perhaps ineffective attempts to interact competently. The positive characterization helps the teacher respond to the child more positively, which in turn increases the chances that the child will have to use and hone his underdeveloped social skills and thereby be provided with the opportunity to break his negative recursive cycle.

In applying this strategy, however, teachers should be careful to remain genuine and authentic in their relationship to the child. We are not recommending the kind of flattery and praise teachers sometimes indulge in to increase a child's self-esteem. Such praise often has a false ring and is counterproductive because it reveals the adult's underlying anxiety about the child's adequacy. The strategy recommended here is a way of appealing to children's good sense.

Teachers' expectations of and attributions to children's characters can have powerful effects on children's behavior. The process of redefining children's characters cannot be "faked" or carried out manipulatively; there are no quick fixes. It takes patience and a genuine—not sentimentalized or phony—consideration of who the child is. If less than authentic, this strategy may be ineffective because many children will see through it. The point is not to manipulate children into feeling good about themselves, but to realize how potent, though often subtle, the expectations, attitudes, attributions, and statements of teachers can be in promoting competence and encouraging acceptance of "difficult children" by the class.

Encouraging impulse control

Satisfying peer relationships are built through use of a variety of social interactive skills that require control over emotions and impulses. The development of such control is one of the major achievements of the preschool period and often needs the support and guidance of parents and teachers. The strategies discussed next can help children in this aspect of development.

It is useful to keep in mind that an optimum amount of order is liberating; too much order and regulation may be stifling and too little may impede realization of the teacher's educational goals and also be stressful for some children. The purpose of rules and routines is to make it possible for the important aspects of classroom life to go smoothly: the pursuit of intellectual, social, physical, aesthetic, and moral learning goals.

While it is never necessary to be mean, to humiliate, to insult, or to belittle children, it is sometimes necessary to be firm or even stern with them—in a one-to-one context. Children are unlikely to be harmed by firmness directed at them by adults who clearly respect them and their feelings and with whom they have established a positive relationship.

Five-year-old Kesha is arguing with her best friend Paul over whose turn it is to ride the class tricycle. Paul stubbornly refuses to yield the tricycle even though Kesha is sure the teacher said it was her turn next. Suddenly Kesha punches Paul in the stomach. Paul, crying, gets off the tricycle and runs to tell his teacher about the altercation.

As in most early childhood classrooms, the children are aware that hitting is banned. After talking to Kesha and Paul, what should their teacher do about this clear violation of a classroom rule? Remove Kesha from the playground? Demand that she sit on the bench until recess is over? Make Kesha apologize to Paul? Tell Kesha that she can't use the tricycle for the rest of the day?

Many teachers (and parents) seem to believe that violation of a rule should invariably be followed by punishment. They may punish the child not so much because they think the behavior warrants it, but because they fear that if they don't respond strongly to the child's misbehavior, the child will not "learn to behave."

Often more effective than punishment is simply discussing the situation with the child. Research has shown that the most effective parental discipline confronts a child's misbehavior in a nonpunitive manner (Maccoby 1980). Young children are more likely to comply with their parents' requests and suggestions (for example, to do chores) when the parents have been responsive to the children's requests, suggestions, and opinions (Parpal & Maccoby 1985). Of particular interest is the finding that children of parents who emphasize discussion and provide simple, straightforward reasons for their disciplinary actions are friendlier than are the children of parents who do not provide reasons with their disciplinary actions (Parpal & Maccoby 1985).

Accommodating individual differences

Early childhood educators have a long-standing tradition of valuing individual differences and autonomy. However, accommodating individual differences can present difficulties. For example, teachers are often reluctant to allow an individual child to opt out of a group activity because other children may also decline to participate.

We have observed incidents in which one child declines to listen to a story with the rest of the class. In such cases the teacher can direct the child to find something else to do that will not disturb the story reading. Teachers have said to us, "But if I let one child opt out, all the others will want to do that, too." In this case the teacher could say, "Fine, let's not

Often more effective than punishment is simply discussing the situation with the child.

have storytime today" or "Let's not have storytime this week" and temporarily drop the activity from the schedule and plan to resume it at a later date. Within a few days the teacher can ask the children whether they would like to resume the activity. If the activity has merit, the children are likely to welcome its resumption.

If most of the children appear disinterested in the activity, a reexamination of its suitability is warranted. If, however, the teacher believes that the activity in question is essential to the children's learning and development, she cannot offer the choice to opt out of it, but must acknowledge respectfully the children's reluctance. She might say calmly and firmly something like, "I know you are not eager to do this, but I think it is very important," and proceed with it.

We suggest that, as long as a nonparticipating child does not present a danger to herself or disrupt the others involved in the activity in question, she should be allowed to have the power to make some of her own decisions, especially if she is shy or self-conscious. If a teacher attempts to coax, cajole, nag, or push individual children into an activity, the entire group of children may feel intimidated or threatened.

For a child who is consistently reluctant to join with classmates, the teacher might take a moment to talk privately with her to determine the real reasons behind the resistance. Together they can design and plan an alternative activity. This strategy can help to reassure the child that the teacher understands and respects her, and misses her when she does not participate. Acknowledging children's feelings reassures them that

they are respected and that help is available when they want or need it. It is important to remember, however, that understanding and respecting children's feelings does not necessarily mean that those feelings should be indulged.

Invoking ground rules

Teachers help create a prosocial atmosphere in the classroom when they indicate that the expectations, limits, and rules invoked apply equally to all children. For example, when the teacher indicates that hitting a playmate is not allowed, she could say something like, "I don't want you to hit Jim, and I don't want anyone to hit you, either." By adding the second part of the statement, the teacher communicates a sense of concern for justice. The message is that the rule invoked to stop the aggressor's behavior will be applied just as faithfully to protect the aggressor should she ever be a victim of that behavior.

Teachers also promote a prosocial class environment when they respond to individual children's needs *as they arise*. A teacher might, for example, respond to a child who is experiencing stress by taking that child on her lap. If others demand a place on it, too, she might say, "Joey is having a really hard time today and needs my special help right now. On a day when you are having a hard time, my lap will be here for you, too."

Some teachers fear that rejection of the second child's request for "lap time" will be perceived as unfair or unequal treatment. Research on parents' socialization of their children's sense of justice (Ross et al. 1990) revealed that parents "instill a sense of justice in their children to the extent that they respect their children's views, clearly explain the logic of their own positions, and emphasize equality" in addressing conflicts (p. 994). We suggest that it is important to distinguish between treating children alike and treating them equitably. Because children's needs, feelings, dispositions, and behavior vary, it would be unfair to treat them all alike.

A healthy social environment is one in which the teacher responds to children's individual differences and needs with equal concern and respect—in other words, equitably. In the second parts of the two teacher statements suggested above, the teacher conveys the idea that the children are in a just environment, one in which all children's needs are addressed with equal seriousness as they arise.

Strengthening prosocial dispositions

Although many children have the knowledge, understanding, and skills required to cope with social situations, the disposition to use the skills may not be sufficiently robust (see Katz 1995). Some children require encouragement to approach social situations such as turn taking and confrontations as problem-solving situations.

For example, young children often complain to the teacher when they cannot get a turn with a desired toy or item of playground equipment. In such situations a useful strategy is for the teacher to ask the complaining child, "What have you tried so far?" They can discuss what approach the child wants to try next to solve the problem. If the child is inexperienced, very hesitant, or not very articulate, the teacher can help by saying something like, "Go back and say, 'I want a turn!' If that doesn't help, let me know, and we can talk about something else to try."

When the teacher offering a suggestion adds, "Let me know, and we can talk about something else to try," she strengthens the child's disposition to approach social situations experimentally without feeling cut off when first efforts are flawed. Without the addendum about considering alternative approaches, if indeed the first suggestion fails, the child's sense of incompetence may be increased.

Appealing to children's good sense

When a teacher gives children responsibility for developing some of the classroom procedures and rules, this signals to the children that the teacher assumes their motives are genuine and that on the whole they are sensible. For example, if children are building a house together and efforts are hampered by too many children working on the construction at the same time, the teacher can suggest that they develop a schedule so that small groups can take turns working on it. If their schedule does not work well, they can evaluate it, discuss its flaws, revise it, and try again.

When adults make most of the decisions and rules governing social participation, they deprive children of opportunities to use their judgment and exercise their good sense and thus to strengthen their dispositions to be responsible and sensible.

Studies of self-attribution processes suggest that when adults address children as though they are capable of approaching social conflicts and problems sensibly, children are apt to

When adults address children as though they are capable of approaching tasks and social conflicts sensibly, children think of themselves as sensible and responsible.

think of themselves as sensible and responsible. Such self-attributions make it more likely that children will use their problem-solving, constructive, and other prosocial dispositions.

Clearly some children are more sensible than others and perhaps more so on some days than others. However, when teachers assume that children are usually motivated to engage in constructive and productive activities, teachers are likely to support and strengthen the children's dispositions to behave responsibly and sensibly.

Helping children cope with adversity

Teachers help to educate children's feelings and emotions by the way the teachers themselves respond to their manifestations (Power 1985; Leavitt & Power 1989). It is one of the teacher's many responsibilities to help children gain emotional perspective and distinguish between what is a tragedy and what is not.

The ability to alter one's emotional response to provocative situations, referred to as *emotion regulation*, begins to develop during the preschool years, and by 6 years of age children generally understand that it is possible to change one's own feelings (Hubbard & Coie 1994). Research suggests that popular boys are better able than unpopular boys to regulate their affect during emotionally arousing play. A classroom climate can become very contentious if its members treat every reversal as a personal tragedy.

For example, young children should not be encouraged to believe that it is a disaster if they miss a turn with a toy. Children do not always have to

get what they want. When one child knocks down another's blocks, it is unfortunate and annoying, but not a disaster; most structures can be rebuilt.

If children make an inordinate fuss about not getting a turn with a toy or about damage accidentally inflicted on their work, the teacher might say, "I know you're disappointed, but there are other things available for you to play with" or "I agree it's annoying when your work is spoiled, but you can do it again." By such statements teachers acknowledge a child's feelings without agreeing that those feelings are appropriate. The use of such statements diminishes the chances of the classroom climate being marked by excessive emotional outbursts and recriminations.

If such incidents occur frequently, then other issues regarding teaching and curriculum have to be considered. Perhaps the curriculum and planned activities are not sufficiently engaging for many of the class members. Other modifications in teaching and curriculum could also be considered that might improve the classroom climate.

Similarly, children do not have to be liked or accepted by all their peers all the time. If individual children complain that another child does not like them, the teacher can acknowledge that this is regrettable, but remind them that they have other friends; or she can let them know that *she* is glad that they are part of the group.

There are events and experiences for which sorrow, sadness, and deep anger are appropriate. For example, when a child is suffering or in real pain, when a friend is moving away, a pet is hurt, or someone is separated from his loved ones, it is appropriate for that child to experience deep sorrow and other

If a child complains that a peer does not like him, the teacher acknowledges his feelings but reminds him that he has other friends and lets him know that she is glad he is part of the group.

strong feelings. Teachers can reassure children that the sadness and anger, though hard to bear, will subside.

Teacher behaviors that undermine social development

The following behaviors, commonplace in classrooms, typically fail to accomplish the teacher's purpose and have unintended negative effects as well.

Issuing empty threats

Adults' credibility can be undermined when they use empty threats in attempting to modify children's behavior. This usually occurs in moments of desperation!

Sometimes teachers threaten children who fail to cooperate in a classroom activity, comply with a rule, or carry their weight regarding classroom responsibilities. Teachers may threaten that the child will not be allowed to enjoy some anticipated special treat.

For example, we observed one teacher who said, "You won't be able to have popcorn with the others later if you don't come to the reading group now." Another said, "If you can't choose a book during our library time, you will have to stay behind when we go to the library next week." In both cases, the teachers had neither the intention nor the disposition to act on their threats.

There are several difficulties with issuing threats. First, it can be hard to make them match the severity of the unwanted behavior. Second, threats are often too difficult to carry out for logistical reasons. Third, many teachers find themselves unable to make the child suffer the promised sanction once the moment of desperation over the incident has passed. For some children threats signal that a teacher's authority is weak; thus her use of threats serves to undermine her credibility.

The underlying principle of this discussion is that communication between teachers and children is likely to be most effective when it is honest, straightforward, respectful. For teachers this means being alert to what they say to children and the possibility of implicit messages that might betray their words.

No doubt mixed messages are part of every culture; after all, culture is largely about elements of feelings,

---

The content of teacher-child interaction should be predominantly related to activities, learning, investigations, and plans.

---

norms, expectations, and patterns of behavior we are usually unaware of until they are violated! Our emphasis on credibility is based on the principle that children thrive on the warmth, acceptance, respect, and praise of someone they look up to—an adult who usually is known to mean what she says.

Making implied comparisons

Teachers often attempt to get a child to attend quietly to a group discussion by using such phrases as "I like the way Lesley is sitting quietly." These phrases tend to be used so frequently that they become clichés. Children understand them as compliments to another child that are intended to alert them to negative evaluations of their own behavior. The implied comparison carries a message to the effect that "I like the way Lesley is behaving but not the way Linda is behaving." This approach is unlikely to build a classroom climate of group solidarity.

We are not suggesting that children should never be encouraged to engage in self-evaluation. Self-evaluation is part of the process of achieving self-regulation (Stipek, Gralinski, & Kopp 1990). However, we wish to note that in our observations of early childhood settings, attempts to coerce appropriate behavior through comparison, when overdone, can create resentment, thus undermining the development of positive and accepting relationships among classmates.

When teachers compliment one child in order to change the behavior of another, children may learn over time that they are in jeopardy when another child is complimented or flattered. They also may learn that their own worth and acceptability are only comparative. This comparative method may teach children to feel that they are being put down when others are being approved. Or they may learn to feel relieved or take comfort in incidents in which classmates are criticized. In addition, some children may become excessively timid in the presence of authority or fearful of being singled out in group situations.

One of the main goals of guidance and limit setting is to help children achieve internal impulse control. An approach that must be used repeatedly with the same children is not achieving its purpose. In other words, if the comparative approach to modifying children's social behavior is used for about the first month of school and it is effective, it would rarely need to be used thereafter. If the teacher must continue to use the method regularly, however, she does so because the strategy has not been effective. Furthermore, although this strategy sometimes works in the short run, it may create resentment and even increase misbehavior in the long run.

The "I-like-the-way-Lesley-is-sitting" approach is designed to modify behavior by comparing children and through the comparison show up faulty behavior. In terms of building a positive classroom ethos, frequent use of this implicitly comparative approach may thwart the development of children's dispositions to take

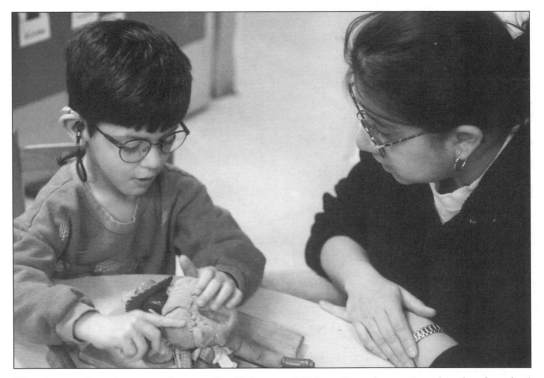

Teacher praise given too frequently distracts children from becoming deeply absorbed in social and intellectual pursuits.

Fostering Children's Social Competence

pleasure in each other's good fortune, gifts, and successes. It is preferable to state matter-of-factly, with calm authority, without rancor or accusation, something like "Please turn around and listen quietly" to the child whose behavior warrants it and then shift the focus to other content.

Our emphasis on matter-of-factness stems from our view that teacher guidance, while it is essential, should not constitute a major focus of teacher-child interaction. Ideally the content of teacher-child interaction should be predominantly issues related to activities, learning, investigations, plans, and so forth. Furthermore, we emphasize matter-of-factness from the conviction that teacher guidance strategies should not be so emotionally loaded that they become distractions in the life of the class.

Using praise inappropriately

Many teachers see the comparative method just discussed primarily as a way of using praise to reinforce desirable behavior. In principle, however, it is best to use praise sparingly. It is doubtful that children benefit from constant flattery and hearing repeatedly that they "did a great job."

For example, we observed a teacher in a class of 4-year-olds who were busy gluing cotton balls on a picture of a lamb. She circled the table where the children were working saying, "Good job! . . . Terrific! . . . Well done! . . . Looks great!" to the point at which it was reasonable to assume that the children had tuned her out! Praise is most effective when it is very specific ("The head of the lamb looks good.") It should be offered just often enough to keep the child encouraged, but not so often that it becomes background noise.

Comments such as "I like the way you helped Annie" may suggest to the children that the teacher does not normally expect helpfulness. It is almost as though the teacher wants to say, "I like the way you helped Annie because I never expected you to." While positive feedback is clearly desirable, it is most likely to be beneficial in amounts optimum (rather than maximum or minimum) for each child.

Some teachers make approving statements to each child in the group to ensure that no one feels left out. With a group of 20 or more children, this practice is a questionable use of time. Again, in most cases, a clear, matter-of-fact statement of the behavior expected and desired should be effective for young children.

In our observation, praise given too frequently is often intrusive and distracts children from becoming deeply absorbed in social and intellectual pursuits. In addition, it teaches children to focus on how well they are doing, particularly in the eyes of others, rather than on what they are doing. In the long term, this practice is associated with weak levels of persistence and lowered self-confidence in children (Dweck & Elliott 1983).

When praise is used too frequently, it is apt to lose its authenticity, meaning, and value; but when it is not used enough, some children may become dispirited and give up trying to meet teacher expectations. Children welcome positive responses from adults they perceive as self-respecting and straightforward.

Posing confusing questions

Teachers sometimes use questions as an indirect way to teach and enforce the rules. The following examples are actual incidents where teachers used questions:

• A teacher responded to a child who demanded a place on her lap during storytime by asking, "How do you think the others will feel when you sit on my lap during storytime?"

• A teacher intervened in a squabble over the use of glue, asking, "How do you think someone feels when you grab his glue?"

• Intervening on behalf of an isolated child, a teacher asked, "Why don't we ask Jake to join us?"

What could the child answer in the first incident? If the child were to say, "I don't care," would the teacher answer, "You should care" or "That's not nice"? Is this exchange constructive? In this incident it was reasonably clear that the child knew how most of the other children would feel if he were on the teacher's lap, but he could not postpone the strong desire to be close to his teacher. Thus it would not help much to hint that the other children would feel envious. It might be more helpful and credible to say calmly and directly, "I know you like sitting on my lap at storytime, but I want you to wait until I've finished" or "I like having you on my lap, but it's hard for me to read and see everyone with someone sitting on my lap."

In the second case, what if the child responded by saying, "He doesn't mind"? How could the teacher respond constructively? What the teacher really wanted to do was indicate that the behavior was inappropriate. By asking a question instead of stating directly what she wanted to communicate, the teacher undermined her credibility, effectiveness, and authority.

Most children involved in such incidents know how the injured party feels, but this knowledge does not regulate their behavior. Asking a child in the heat of the moment how others might feel when their rights, desires, or needs are disregarded is often counterproductive because it may embarrass the child and sometimes undermine his self-confidence. While it may not hurt to urge a child to consider how others might feel in some similar contexts, it would be more helpful to remind the child that the next time he needs the glue, he can check with the others to find out if they have finished with it or simply ask the others for a turn to use it.

If a child's communication skills are weak, the teacher can suggest an appropriate phrase to use. If a particular child is involved frequently in such incidents, it might help to stay close during situations in which the proprietary behavior is likely to occur and to intervene with firm and clear suggestions of alternative strategies.

In the third example, when the teacher asks, "Why don't we ask Jake to join us?" the children may say "No" or "He's weird" or "We don't like him." It would be more effective for the teacher to say, "I think it would be a good idea to ask Jake to join us." Although the children might still disagree and give their reasons, the teacher has clearly, honestly, and credibly expressed her view of what she believes to be the desirable action.

A similar problem arises when teachers ask children who are squabbling about such things as taking turns with equipment, "What could we have done about this?" or "What could you have said, Johnny?" or "What words could you have used?" These are interrogatories—questions to which the questioner already knows the answers. They put children under pressure to come up with the answer the teacher wants and they can make respondents feel defensive. While the teacher's intention to remind children to use verbal approaches to resolve conflicts is appropriate, these essentially rhetorical questions are too indirect. Furthermore, such questions are frequently condescending, phony, or unreal, and children realize when a teacher is talking down to them.

Attributing needs to children excessively

We have observed a similar pattern when teachers make statements to children such as "You need to sit down" or "You need to wait until I call your name." Although most children understand the teacher's real message in these cases, we question the wisdom of attributing needs to children. It can be condescending when someone tells others what their needs are; it can also be intimidating or threatening. We suggest that the teacher instead state her desire directly by saying something like, "Please sit down" or "I want you to sit down now" or "Please wait until your name is called."

Similarly, we have observed teachers using such phrases as "I need you to sit down" or "I need you to turn around." The behavior desired by the teacher is clear in these statements, but it seems unnecessary and inappropriate for teachers to allude frequently to their own "needs." It would be more

straightforward to request the desired behavior in a simple and direct statement such as, "Please sit down."

Let us take the opportunity to reiterate that none of these daily incidents requires strong affect or high intensity. They are best approached with quiet, calm authority so that the really important events of group life can proceed smoothly.

Motivating children by indirect disapproval

Teachers and parents often try to motivate children by implying that undesirable behavior means they belong elsewhere. For example, we observed a teacher chiding a first grader by saying, "You're not in kindergarten now." This approach is risky because it may undermine children's capacities to respond charitably to less mature children. How could a first grader who has been criticized for exhibiting kindergarten behavior be expected to develop a nurturing and helpful approach to kindergartners? Indeed, it may encourage them to take comfort from others' troubles. This strategy may also teach children to become disdainful of their own earlier efforts rather than taking pride in where they so recently came from.

In this case, a clear statement or description of the desired behavior is preferable. We suggest further that instead of putting a child down in this way, teachers strive to create a classroom and school climate in which children learn to regard younger children in a positive light. In such a climate children can learn to take delight in seeing how far they have progressed while accepting and respecting where their younger peers still are.

Using time-out inappropriately

Informal observation indicates that time-out or sitting in the "thinking chair" is a strategy commonly used by teachers for children who violate classroom norms, particularly by being aggressive. Anecdotal evidence suggests that the thinking chair is used excessively and ineffectively and in ways that can demean children. Furthermore, young children's understanding of the connection between being told to sit on a particular chair and the incident that led to it may be vague at best! We have found no research that describes what children think about when they are sent to the thinking chair (or, at home, to their room) to think about their unacceptable behavior. If the thinking chair or time-out is used repeatedly for the same few chil-

dren, its effectiveness in developing a child's capacity for impulse control is questionable. To consider the thinking chair a generic solution to curbing aggressive outbursts supports the assumption that punishment is always the most effective response to unwarranted aggression.

One of the risks of time-out procedures is that they may give rise to thoughts of revenge and perhaps even cultivate children's taste for it. Furthermore, time-out used as punishment may humiliate children. These procedures also violate the principle of acknowledging and respecting children's feelings.

Another major disadvantage of using time-out as punishment is that it does not teach a child alternative ways of responding to the situation at hand. It is therefore unlikely to strengthen

Using time-out as a punishment may humiliate and anger the child; moreover, it does not teach the child alternative ways of dealing with the situation.

Fostering Children's Social Competence

social skills. In fact, punitive time-out procedures often distract both the child and the teacher from the difficult processes of learning how to solve problems in social relationships. For the teacher, the problem is how to help a child change what is often a chronic tendency to behave in self-defeating, irritating ways that disrupt the rest of the class. From the child's point of view, her disruptive behavior usually leads to rejection by others and painful and difficult interaction with peers.

The child and the teacher can both benefit from resolving the problem and ending a cycle of misbehavior and punishment that may reinforce the child's tendency to misbehave rather than change it for the better. Ironically, then, such time-out procedures as sitting in the thinking chair often reinforce the child's tendency to flout the rules rather then help her to comply.

An appropriate use of time-out is to withdraw disruptive children from the flow of action they are unable to manage so that they will calm down and regain control over their impulses. Such withdrawal, which is very much like time-out in a basket-ball game, is not intended as punishment. The teacher might explain to a child, "Jane, I think a few minutes of rest until you are not quite so angry with Jill is a good idea. Then the two of you can figure out how you can both have a turn on the slide. Let me know when you're ready to work things out. I'll be glad to help if you would like." This strategy should be free of any hint of punishment. It is not necessary to provide a particular chair that can humiliate or shame the child, much like being made to wear a dunce cap or stand in the corner.

* * *

In this chapter we examined teaching strategies effective in fostering social competence, and we identified a number of teacher behaviors—very common in early childhood classrooms—that may do more harm than good. Next we look at components of social competence that are important for children to develop throughout childhood, and what teachers can do to promote this development.

5

Strengthening Specific Components of Social Competence

Extensive research comparing well-liked children with those who are less liked indicates that social knowledge, social understanding, and interactive skills, along with the disposition to use these competencies, play a significant role in initiating and maintaining successful relations with peers (Gottman 1983). In this chapter we discuss teaching approaches to address specifically these two components of social competence.

Fostering social knowledge and understanding

Many children need adult help from time to time in coming to understand that peers may have experiences, backgrounds, desires, family routines, and points of view different from their own. The following discussion covers techniques that teachers can use to bring about fuller social knowledge and understanding in children to assist them in building social relationships.

Arousing empathy and altruism

Many situations provide an opportunity to evoke and reinforce children's empathic and altruistic dispositions. Suppose, for example, that a child has been waiting a long time for a turn on a piece of outdoor play equipment. When the teacher feels that the child who is using the equipment should yield it to the child who is waiting, she can say calmly, "Robin has been waiting a long time, and you know how it feels to wait." The second part of the statement is made in a straightforward manner that conveys no attribution of meanness, shame, or other negative implication.

Along the same lines, it may be particularly important in the case of aggressive children to help them deepen their understanding of the effects of their actions on other children and of others' feelings in difficult situations. In such cases a teacher can indicate privately to the child her view of how others react to his or her actions. The commonly used approach of saying,

"How would you like it if someone did that to you?" is not likely to be as effective as a firm and clear statement such as, "I am sure Bill doesn't like it when you do that to him. Try another way to tell him what you mean."

Alerting children to others' feelings and interests

In appropriate contexts it is helpful for adults to alert children to others' feelings and interests. The goal is to develop children's dispositions to speculate and anticipate the responses and feelings of peers to various events, thereby deepening their knowledge and understanding of others. In the course of a discussion about plans for a forthcoming activity, for example, a teacher can ask one child or several children what they think an absent child might prefer or how that child might react to the plans developed thus far.

This use of the interrogatory form differs from the example discussed in Chapter 4 where the teacher asked, "How do you think the others would feel if I let you sit on my lap?" That example is an indirect attempt by the teacher to decline the child's request and is not intended to develop understanding and insight. The teacher's questions here are intended to stimulate and strengthen children's dispositions to anticipate others' feelings and to be aware of others' interests. When teachers raise these issues, they convey the idea that sensitivity to others' opinions, interests, and feelings is important and valued.

Teachers can also model the disposition to anticipate others' feelings and interests. A teacher can discuss with children his own conjectures concerning what children in another class might want to know about the work going on in his class, or how others might be able to give them ideas or assistance in a project they are working on.

In a class of 4-year-olds, we observed a good example of a teacher fostering children's dispositions to speculate on others' feelings and interests. The teacher talked with her class about four absent children who were expected to move to another school after the holidays and so would no longer be their classmates. She began the discussion by telling the 4-year-olds which children would not be returning and saying, "I think it would be nice if our class gave them something to help them remember their time with us. Any ideas about what we could do?" Half of the group offered suggestions about what they thought the departing children were most interested in; most of the other children reacted thoughtfully to the suggestions offered. The discussion ended with general agreement that the children should prepare a painting for each of their departing classmates to hang in his or her new home.

Further discussion led the children to divide themselves into four groups, with each group producing a picture for one of the departing classmates. The teacher then led the class in a discussion of what they thought each of the four children had found most memorable about his or her experience in the class. The class shared their recollections of their four classmates' interests, favorite field trips, and so forth. The pictures that the groups enthusiastically produced were delightfully detailed and personalized.

On this particular occasion the teacher used an unusual circumstance to create a context in which she could repeatedly invite the children to predict and reflect on their peers' feelings and interests. The discussions culminated in successful group projects illustrating their recollections.

This approach will work not just for unusual events or crises but in any context in which a variety of feelings and opinions are present.

Encouraging alternative interpretations of others' behavior

Sometimes children assign negative labels to peers who are different or difficult or whom they dislike. They may try to assign a nickname like "weirdo," "nerd," "crybaby," "sissy," or some other favorite insult. Teachers can cul-

tivate a constructive social environment to discourage labelers by asking them to consider other ways of interpreting the labeled child's behavior. The teacher might, for example, mention that the child is new to the class, neighborhood, or country; or she might explain that the child's family does things differently from theirs, and that that is all right. The teacher is also making it clear by what she says and how she says it that she herself accepts and respects the child and his ways.

Whether the teacher happens upon a correct reinterpretation of the labeled child's behaviors or characteristics is not as important as is her urging children to consider alternative interpretations of others' behavior. The teacher's intervention does not require a high level of affect, but a calm and firm assertion of her point of view. The

Recognizing that young children are capable of concern for others, teachers can take action to strengthen children's empathetic feelings and actions.

important points for the teacher to communicate are that she expects the children to think about reasons for the differences among their classmates, that she accepts the differences, and that she expects the children to accept and respect the differences.

Similarly, chronically aggressive children can often be helped to find alternative interpretations of the intentions prompting others' behavior. Aggressive children are often quick to attribute aggressive intentions to others. Evidence suggests that helping them explore alternative attributions of the intentions behind others' disruptive behavior can help children gain perspective and reduce their tendency to respond with anger (Hudley & Graham 1993).

> *Five-year-old Rick trips and falls into a block structure that Kintu is building. Kintu's demeanor shows anger and a readiness to strike out against Rick. However, Rick, a particularly skillful classmate, says instantly, "Sorry, Kintu, I tripped and it was an accident. Let me help you fix it." Kintu's face and hands immediately relax, and he reveals his acceptance of Rick's true intentions with a smile.*

Upon disrupting Kintu's block play, Rick interprets his own actions to Kintu as unintentional, thus defusing a stressful situation. Many children spontaneously arrive at nonhostile interpretations of the potentially threatening behavior of a peer without an explanation from the other child or the intervention of a teacher.

In other cases, the teacher needs to help a child recognize that another person's intention was not aggressive. She can do this by pointing out that not all disruptions are deliberate and that the children can negotiate, resolve their conflict, and resume their activities. Learning to consider peers' intentions may take time for some children, but it will serve them well in future social interactions.

Helping children participate appropriately in ongoing discussions

From time to time a child will disrupt large or small group discussions or group work by making comments unrelated to the situation—behavior sometimes referred to as "off-the-wall." Unfortunately, such a child may readily be labeled by peers as "weird" or in other ways strange. In this type of out-of-sync behavior the teacher can assist the child in gaining the knowledge and understanding of social situations necessary for more appropriate participation in group discussions and similar social situations.

In some cases such behavior is the result of an insufficiently developed ability to read social situations accurately, which leads to comments that are off the subject. In other cases the child may change the subject because she cannot contribute to the one under discussion and feels left out. Sometimes children's comments seem to be off the topic because they are way ahead of their peers on the subject being discussed and lack patience with those behind them.

In the first two cases the teacher can confer individually with the child, offering specific suggestions about topics that are pertinent and of interest to others in the group. For example, she might explain to the child that while not everyone in the class is interested in collecting stamps, many would be very eager to hear about her new puppy. Or, based on the teacher's knowledge of the hobbies or recent experiences of some of the children, and knowing that these children would respond positively to a show of interest by the child, the teacher might suggest, "I think it would be a good idea to ask Warren about his trip with his family in their camper last week."

In the third case the teacher can encourage the child to be more patient and at the same time can acknowledge the child's feelings by indicating that it is sometimes hard to wait when a discussion is going slowly. The teacher's remarks should not be heavy-handed, nor should they imply that the impatient child is in any way selfish or mean.

In all three cases the teacher can encourage the children to listen quietly to others when they are part of a group situation.

Helping children discover common ground

Developing friendships often blossom when would-be friends discover interests, experiences, or preferences they hold in common (Gottman 1983). A teacher can prime the pump by indicating interests or experiences one child holds in common with another child. These shared interests may form the basis of a solid friendship. For example, a teacher might say to a child, "Jenny also collects shells; she might like to see your new one" or "Jimmy is interested in dinosaurs, too." When a child is eager to share news about a trip to the children's museum, the teacher might say, "Don't forget to tell Jean about what you saw; she went there last week." Or, in another case, she can say, "Ron also has a baby brother who gets into his toys."

In this way the teacher does not have to be the recipient of every piece of news; she can build strong community feelings by encouraging cross-child exchange when appropriate.

Encouraging constructive feedback among children

This approach is consistent with a more general one of referring children to one another so that they develop the disposition to share thoughts and feelings and to recount experiences to each other. For example, a teacher might suggest to one child that he take some time before the end of the day to look at something another child has written or made and discuss his views of the item with the child who created it. This practice can foster a habit of spontaneous child-to-child interaction so that children do not always have to direct their communication to or through adults.

Strengthening interactive skills

In helping children to strengthen the skills essential to social competence, one of the most important teaching strategies is to give children ample opportunity to interact about meaningful matters in the course of each day—during play, work, and, when appropriate, transitions. Just as children learn to ride a bicycle by riding a bicycle, so they develop social skillfulness by engaging in social interaction. Opportunities for social interaction are thought of by some parents, and even some educators, as a frivolous or peripheral part of the school day and a break from "real work." To the contrary, social interaction around substantive content is one of the most, if not *the* most, critical factors in optimum cognitive development (Rogoff 1990).

One reason it is important to help children establish positive relationships in the early years is that a child who is rejected by her peers, or is thwarted in some other way in learning the social ropes from peers, has lost a very important source of social information.

In a study in which Japanese preschool teachers analyzed videotapes of American preschool classrooms, the Japanese preschool teachers were consistently struck by the lengths to which American teachers go to protect children from the disapproval or anger of their peers (Tobin, Wu, & Davidson 1989). The Japanese teachers held that disapproval by peers often provides children with information about what behavior needs to be changed and how to go about changing it. While it is never necessary or sound to allow children to be cruel to one another, there may be times when the most effective way to help a child change behavior that others find objectionable is to allow the child the opportunity to work things out among her peers.

Fostering verbal communication

Verbal skills play a critical role in social interaction even in the early years. Teachers can help children develop verbal skills by indicating ways in which they can state clearly their feelings, desires, and ideas.

The teacher's knowledge of each child provides a basis on which she can offer suggested phrases at the ap-

propriate level of complexity. For one child the suggestion might be, "Say to Ann, 'Please pass me that crayon'" or "Say to Thomas, 'I want to use the paintbrush a bit longer.'" For another child the suggestion might be, "Let Jimmy know that it bothers you when he makes the table shake." In some cases it is useful to suggest topics for conversation. The specificity of the suggestions offered should depend on the teacher's assessment of the child's competencies.

Some teachers have reported to us great success in helping children whose speech is unclear by teaching the whole class to use sign language. In this way the children are able to interact smoothly with others, and the knowledge and skills gained by all members of the class can serve them well in other life situations. Based on these teachers' reports, most children enjoy learning this special way of interacting with adults and peers.

Offering suggestions for verbal openings

Sometimes children can enter ongoing play groups more easily when they use an opening gambit. Depending on the child, the teacher can offer suggestions that are indirect or very specific.

As we stated earlier, if individual children are making good progress in verbal interactive skills, the teacher can discuss with them what they have tried thus far and what they think they might try next. A teacher taking a more indirect approach could suggest that the child ask other children what they are planning, doing, or making. Children can also ask how they might be able to help.

Fostering Children's Social Competence

Social interaction around substantive content is one of the most critical factors in optimum cognitive development.

In the case of a child with few verbal skills who is just getting started in interactive play, the teacher can be more direct. Suggestions could include statements such as, "Go to Jane and say, 'May I work on this side of the building?'" The teacher can model the appropriate tone of voice for the request.

It should be noted that approaches to groups are more likely to be successful if the child approaching makes positive comments about what the group is doing.

Strengthening turn-taking skills

A common complaint young children bring to their teachers is that another child will not allow them to play with a particular object or on a piece of equipment that is in short supply. As suggested in Chapter 3, such situations are best defined as issues of turn taking rather than sharing.

A large part of social interaction requires turn taking. Conversations, discussions, and carrying one's weight in the household duties, for example, all involve some form of coordinated turn taking. Turn taking involves being able to detect cues in a partner's behavior that indicate that he is about to bring his turn to an end, to discern the moment that would be the most propitious to press for one's own turn, and so forth. Mastery of these skills takes time and lots of experience.

Turn-taking problems, as we have noted, are often resolved when the teacher encourages the child to return to the situation and ask for a turn. "If this request does not work," the teacher adds, "come back and we will consider another approach." If reasonable requests are to no avail, the teacher can step in and remind the resisting child that others are waiting.

Such incidents sometimes provide an appropriate context for evoking a child's capacity for empathy and altruism, as we discussed at the beginning of this chapter. Again the teacher might say, "You know how it feels to wait a long time for a turn." The basic strategy is to appeal to the resisting child's capacity for generosity and good sense. If this approach fails, the teacher can intercede after a suitable waiting period by offering, without rancor, a simple explanation such as, "I think Robin has waited long enough." The explanation can be followed with a friendly chat about other activities the child might find of interest. This will prevent such incidents from becoming significant content in the resisting child's relationship with the teacher.

Helping children develop negotiating skills

Many aspects of social interaction require negotiation among participants as to the sequence, structure, and general give-and-take of the interaction. Successful negotiation involves being able to guess with a fair degree of accuracy what will appeal to another child and being able to work out a deal in which each participant's preferences or needs are considered (Rubin & Everett 1982). It is likely

Children benefit from help in developing skills for negotiating and compromising.

that sociometric status and skill in developing compromises are related to each other.

Children benefit from help in developing skills for negotiating and compromising. Teachers can offer phrases that the children could use and suggest some bargains that could be struck. For example, a teacher could suggest to one child that he say to another child, "I'll pull you in the wagon if you push me on the swing afterward."

Teaching children to assert their preferences gracefully

Well-liked children are more able than their less-liked peers to reduce tension in play by offering reasons for their preferences and insistence on their points of view (Gottman 1983). Sometimes a teacher can help by suggesting reasons a child

might give for insisting on his stance in a conflict.

When popular children were compared with unpopular children, the former were found to use a softened form of rejection when resisting the efforts of other children to play or direct their activity. This approach to de-escalating tension in interaction requires children to give a reason for their resistance to peers' demands. Researchers found that popular children give tactful rejections to their peers' requests and demands (Hazen, Black, & Fleming-Johnson 1982). Such a rejection might be expressed with words like, "I can't play right now because I already started this game, but maybe later, OK?" A squabble about who is to play the role of waitress might be defused when the insistent child says, "I have to be the waitress because my mommy is one!"

Fostering Children's Social Competence

Helping to minimize teasing

Teasing and taunting are common experiences of childhood. Teasing is generally defined as persistent behavior intended to irritate, provoke, confuse, or otherwise annoy someone, such as assigning a peer an insulting nickname that refers to an undesirable or unusual attribute.

It is surprising to us that teasing behavior is rarely, if ever, mentioned in the extensive research literature on social development. The fourth volume of the 1983 edition of the *Handbook of Research on Child Development* (Hetherington 1983), devoted to research on socialization, personality, and social development, does not list either bullying or teasing in the subject index of the contents of its more-than-one-thousand pages! Nevertheless, teasing and similar unkind behavior among peers is one of children's most frequently cited concerns (Johnson 1986).

In some cultures teasing is associated with relationships marked by particularly close bonding (Ervin-Tripp 1989). This suggests that there may be a positive side to mutual teasing in some relationships. It raises the questions, Are there any potential benefits to learning to tease and to being teased? Is the capacity to cope with the give-and-take of a teasing relationship an indicator of social competence? Anecdotal evidence from extensive experience with suicidal adolescents indicates that one of their characteristics is an inability to laugh at themselves (Cooney 1996). It is not known, however, whether this inability stems from excessive or insufficient experience in being teased during childhood. It may be that an optimum amount of being teased in childhood provides a basis for competence later in coping with interpersonal difficulties. Research on these issues is greatly needed.

We do not know why some children seem relatively warm and lighthearted during teasing incidents, while others respond with pain and humiliation. Japanese teachers believe that children developing social skills must experience some of the bumps and barbs inflicted in the course of interaction with peers. Japanese teachers are watchful but reluctant to intervene; their assumption is that children need to learn to stand up for themselves, and also that the child's peer group may step in to stop hostile behavior when it seems to be too severe (Tobin, Wu, & Davidson 1989).

Clearly some teasers are more malicious than others, and the question of when to intervene depends on the adults' judgment of the victim's distress as well as the level of hostility of the teaser. We suggest that teachers can help best by carefully observing teasing among children and considering several conditions when deciding whether to intervene:

• **Context:** Does the teasing occur during play with a friend, or does the teasing occur in front of a group?

• **Source:** What is the relationship between the teaser and the teased? Are they members of the same friendship group?

• **Mutuality:** Are there indications of reciprocal teasing? Is the teasing mutual among members of a group rather than focused on one victim?

• **Tone and intention:** Is the tone of the teasing warm in expression and reception? Is there humor in the content or style of the teasing? Or is the tone hostile with an apparent intention to inflict psychological pain?

When a teacher considers the conditions and decides that real pain and harm are occurring, he can use one of several strategies listed earlier in this chapter. For example, the teacher might say, "Paula, I don't want you to talk to Brian that way, and I don't want anyone to talk to you that way either." Or the teacher can suggest to Brian that he say clearly and firmly to Paula that he doesn't like to be teased, advising Brian to return to him for further advice if that does not help. The teacher can make these suggestions clearly in a reassuring and matter-of-fact tone

that does not imply in any way that he believes the child worthy of taunting or particularly vulnerable.

If the teasing carries overtones of racism, sexism, or any stereotyping, the teacher can address the larger issue directly with the children involved and possibly with their parents. On some occasions he might discuss possible centerwide or schoolwide steps with the appropriate administrator.

As in other aspects of peer interaction, the educational contexts we create for and with children may also influence the extent to which teasing occurs. A study of Swedish child care centers found that in classrooms with a wide variety of interesting things to

Children who are chronically aggressive or bullying should be distinguished from those who engage in rough-and-tumble play.

Fostering Children's Social Competence

do, children are less likely to engage in teasing or rejection of one another (Ekholm & Hedin 1985).

Helping bullies and their victims change their behaviors

Even in the preschool period there are children capable of making their peers do things against their will or preventing them from exercising their will. Boys who fit this pattern are usually labeled "bullies" while girls are described as "bossy." The teacher is concerned not only with helping the bullying children to modify their behavior but also with enabling other children to resist them.

While bullies seem to be strong and to get what they want in their social interactions, they may nevertheless feel unlikable and suffer from low self-esteem. Children who are persistently aggressive are usually a problem to themselves as well as to others. This behavior pattern correlates strongly with low sociometric standing among peers. It is highly stable over time and predictive of later life difficulties (Parker & Asher 1987). In fact, the most highly stable behavioral traits are those found among children described as "disruptive" and "starters of fights" (Coie & Dodge 1983). Children rejected for these behaviors seldom outgrow them spontaneously.

Children who are chronically aggressive or who bully other children should be distinguished from those who are appropriately assertive in defending their rights or who engage in a certain amount of rough-and-tumble play. In addition, a transitory period of more pronounced aggressiveness may be a step toward maturity for a child who has yielded passively to others'

assertions or withdrawn habitually to adult protection. Because aggression carries a high price in terms of peer rejection and adult disapproval, it is usually discarded by such a child in favor of more mature techniques (Maccoby 1980).

But aggression also carries some short-term benefits and so is not always discarded. One study notes that three-quarters of aggressive acts by one preschool child against another are met with positive consequences for the aggressor; that is, the aggressor gets what she wants. Furthermore, when the aggressor succeeds, the chances of her using the same method in the future increases (Maccoby 1980). The child who continues to use aggression as a tool and fails to adopt more mature techniques within a short period needs help in breaking a potentially dangerous cycle.

Helping the bully. Some bullying children may be motivated to change their behavior if they are helped to make the connection between their low social status and their aggressiveness. Others require direct teacher intervention in curbing their aggressive impulses and in understanding how their behavior affects others.

Teachers often attempt to modify bullying behavior by asking the bully questions such as, "How would you like someone to do that to you?" Questions of this nature require analysis and reflection beyond the capabilities of the young child. In addition, they have an element of inauthenticity. Do we expect the child to answer, "It would offend me greatly"? Such questions usually yield a noncommittal response like, "I don't care."

Instead, the teacher might indicate to the bullying child that she does not like his behavior because it is not fun to be pushed around. Furthermore, she would not want anyone to push him around either.

Helping the victim. Most children can probably benefit from help in handling a bully at one time or another. Some children, however, have particular difficulty in standing up to bullies. There is increasing awareness of the role of the victim in bully-victim relationships (Dodge & Coie 1989). Bullies are not randomly aggressive toward other children but frequently have favorite victims. Research on groups of boys at play indicates that some boys develop a reputation for being easy marks among their male peers "because they consistently reinforce the aggressive actions of their peers with submission" (Schwartz, Dodge, & Coie 1993, 1756; Slaby et al. 1995).

We recommend a twofold approach to helping victims. First, teachers can show children who are being victimized how to respond to the bully with composure. If victims respond pugnaciously, they will surely fail because this is the bully's preferred style of interaction. Furthermore, counter-aggression sanctions this kind of interaction. Teachers can suggest to potential victims that, instead of submitting to the bully, they can resist him calmly.

Second, depending on the social competence of the victims, the teacher can suggest that they let the aggressive child know how they feel about him. For potential victims who are less articulate, the teacher can offer a phrase to use and can model the composed but assertive tone in which to say it. The teacher could suggest to a child who protests being pushed, "Say to Robin, 'I don't like to be pushed!'" The teacher should not give into the temptation to tell the victim to just give the bully what he deserves! The teacher could also explain to the bully how the victim feels, being sure not to imply that the teacher rejects the aggressor. If this twofold approach fails, the teacher must step in more firmly to reduce the bullying behavior as it unfolds.

Providing opportunities for social interaction by pairing children

In some cases it is useful to pair a less-liked child with a more popular child (but not the most popular one) to undertake a particular task. The teacher can make such pairings without hinting to the more popular child that he or she is doing a good turn and deserves a pat on the back! By making such teams the teacher conveys the expectation that the two children will work together to complete the task. If the more popular child protests, the teacher can acknowledge the protest matter-of-factly but insist firmly that the assignment be carried out. The teacher's insistence conveys to the children involved, and possibly to anyone observing from the sidelines, that she expects children to work together even if they are not best friends, and that children do not necessarily have to like each other to work together. Frequently children's (and adult's) initial reluctance recedes as they work or play with people they know less well or to whom they are not attracted and they get to know each other.

Another possibility is to pair an older child with a younger child—for

Teachers can show children who are being victimized how to respond with composure to the bully.

Strengthening Specific Components of Social Competence

example, a 5-year-old with a 3- or 4-year-old. Because the 5-year-old does not feel the need to compete for dominance with or outshine the younger child, she can practice her social skills and often enhance them significantly. Such a pairing can be advantageous if the older child is having problems in social relationships with same-age peers. The older child may feel less threatened by the younger child and open up to him in ways that do not occur with same-age peers. As we have already suggested, cross-age pairing can be a more powerful intervention than other forms of intervention such as individual therapy, talking with the child, or pairing with a same-age peer (Suomi & Harlow 1975; Hartup 1983).

Providing alternatives to tattling

From time to time a teacher is confronted with a child who seeks attention through tattling or telling tales about other children's misdeeds. Instead of acting on the information offered, the teacher can advise the child to go back and remind the others about the rules. Again, this suggestion is best made in a straightforward and matter-of-fact way.

In a pilot study with kindergarten children, tattling behavior was correlated moderately with aggressive behavior (McClellan 1989). Anecdotal evidence indicated that children who tattle about one another tend to respond aggressively to conflict and to tell tales about others at higher-than-average rates. Both tendencies might be related to ineffective strategies for dealing with conflict; however, in some cases telling tales relates highly to needs for adult attention or approval.

By the time children are 7 or 8 years old, teachers can help them understand that they should inform the teacher about another's behavior when that person is endangering herself or others or damaging property. During the preschool and kindergarten years, however, children usually are not yet able to recognize such instances reliably, and adults must accept total responsibility for monitoring where children are and what they are doing.

Providing social skill training

There are often occasions when it is appropriate for teacher and child to discuss a chronic behavior problem away from its context, when neither is feeling defensive or angry about it. Rather than confronting, lecturing, or punishing children in the heat of the moment, the teacher might make a mental note of the behavior. Later, when tempers have cooled, the teacher can conduct an "intervention mini-session" with the relevant child or small group of children. She can explain the ramifications of their behavior and help them develop alternative approaches. This strategy is often referred to by researchers and practitioners as *social skill training* (Cartledge & Fellows-Milburn 1980; Shure 1992).

Effectiveness of social skill training

Social skill training might be thought of as the process of making explicit those unwritten rules of social interaction that are usually learned informally and unconsciously. The essence of social skill training procedures is in their *metacognitive* nature: behaviors that usually remain unconscious are opened up for scrutiny, and behavior patterns that tend to pit children against adults in an unconscious tug-of-war become more conscious and therefore more easily modified.

A small but influential group of researchers (Gottman & Schuler 1976; Hymel & Asher 1977; Oden & Asher 1977; Ladd 1983; Bierman & Furman 1984; Coie & Krehbiel 1984; Gresham & Nagle 1984; LaGreca & Santogrossi 1984; Mize & Ladd 1990) has addressed a variety of behaviors (conversation skills, group entry skills, control of aggression, and so forth) and examined the effectiveness of systematically teaching some children what others seem to grasp intuitively. Results have been encouraging, indicating not only positive changes in the children's behavior but also marked positive changes in the children's popularity that are sustained over time (see Mize & Ladd 1990). For example, one study found that preschoolers who have brief and nonjudgmental discussions with their teacher about the consequences of positive and negative social behavior subsequently engage in significantly less aggressive behavior and are better liked by their classmates (Zahavi & Asher 1978).

In another study, researchers taught somewhat socially isolated third-grade children the nuts and bolts of participating and communicating socially with other children. At the end of several brief sessions, previously isolated children were found to be more skillful with and better accepted by their peers. In follow-up assessments, gains in social skillfulness and peer acceptance were sustained (Gresham & Nagle 1984).

Guidelines in social skill training

Teachers who wish to help children change ineffective behavior might consider the following three aspects as guidelines:

1. Knowledge: Does the child know what she needs to know to be socially effective? Does she know, for example, that other children are more likely to allow an additional playmate into an ongoing group activity if that child waits quietly at the sidelines for a few moments before trying to jump in?

2. Action: Is the child able to practice and act in accordance with this knowledge?

3. Application: Is the child able to apply her knowledge in most social settings? If she has learned a new skill, is she likely to apply it in future interactions? (Mize & Ladd 1990)

The teaching process

Acting out new social understanding helps the learner (and teacher) identify points not fully understood before. In addition, enacting a behavior increases the likelihood that it will be recalled later. Sometimes the enactment of the desired behavior may be more successful when small dolls are used, especially with younger children. One study found that 5-year-old children who were shy about role-playing or acting out a behavior with a teacher were much more comfortable when child and teacher used dolls or puppets as surrogates. This was particularly true when the behavior at issue involved aggression (McClellan 1989).

In such cases it can be helpful to remind the child to try the suggested

> *Like an apprentice, a child learns from more experienced peers and adults through observation, coaching, and practice.*

strategy in the course of his interaction with others. Reminders are more likely to be effective when offered unobtrusively, tactfully, and nonjudgmentally. Sometimes the teacher and child can agree in advance on an unobtrusive signal to remind the child of the behavior change she is working on so as not to cause embarrassment in front of other children. The idea is to establish an atmosphere of warmth, support, and collaboration in which teacher and child work together to change the targeted behavior.

For example, a kindergarten teacher notices that Josh, a child in her class, is often rebuffed by other children. She believes that this happens partly because he approaches others awkwardly. The teacher waits until she can find a quiet moment with Josh, then she suggests that he try watching quietly from the sidelines before attempting to enter an ongoing group activity. Her demeanor is that of a coach rather than that of an instructor as she discusses with Josh ways that well-liked children gain group entry.

To further the child's ability to take action, the teacher engages Josh briefly in role-playing the desired behavior.

Finally, to help him remember to apply the strategy, she and Josh develop a signal that she will give him when she notices him trying to join an ongoing play group. She also suggests to him that he try to remember the strategy without the signal.

Parents and teachers use this approach intuitively when they discuss informally with children the benefits of saying, for example, "Excuse me" or "I beg your pardon" in appropriate situations. In such cases we are teaching children the social conventions that facilitate smooth, peaceful, and efficient human interaction.

Maria Montessori (1964) observed that children were often embarrassed and hurt needlessly simply because they did not know a particular social convention appropriate to the situation. For example, she noticed that many of the children she worked with were unfamiliar with the conventions used when one sneezes, which caused them embarrassment and adult disapproval. After presenting a little lesson on this topic, she reported being astonished at the care and dignity with which the children carried out the procedure.

The success of this approach supports the concept of children as apprentices to older or more experienced persons (Rogoff 1990). Like an apprentice, a child learns from more experienced peers and adults through observation, coaching, and contextually embedded practice.

Limitations of social skill training

The usefulness of social skill training interventions depends on many factors, including the child's age and metacognitive skill (that is, his capacity to reflect on his own behaviors and interactions). It is important to note that such interventions should not be considered cure-alls. Social interactions are complex phenomena that are often resistant to the most thoughtful attempts to change them.

Packer and Richardson (1989), for example, offer a case study of a preschooler who did many of the "right things" when seeking entry to groups and playing with others, but whose behavior, nevertheless, was out of sync with that of her peers. As a result, other children did not like her. As Packer and Richardson suggest, there may be a total organization to a child's behavior that is not easily altered by the addition of a few discrete skills. After all, social interaction patterns—effective and ineffective ones—are integrated into an individual's personality organization, which cannot be entirely transformed by separate, fragmented subskills training.

Throughout this discussion our assumption is that effective teaching, though guided by knowledge of the components of social skillfulness, does not inevitably result from carrying out specific or isolated prescriptions for child or teacher change, no matter how credible the source. Rather, the appropriateness of a response to a particular incident or behavior can be determined only by trial and error and by patient observation of the whole pattern of the child's interactions with others.

* * *

We have outlined a variety of approaches to help teachers strengthen components of children's social competence. Some address the range of common social difficulties teachers of young children inevitably encounter, and others address specific difficulties. As far as we know, nothing works for all children, and all of the approaches we have recommended can be overdone!

Many children with social difficulties require specialized help that goes beyond that which the classroom teacher can provide. However, we know from our own experience and the experiences of many of our students who teach young children that spending a little time alone with a child—perhaps 10 minutes a day for a week or two—can often help the child make a big step in a positive direction. The time spent alone with the teacher, doing something simple and pleasurable, often serves to reassure the child that the teacher really cares about her. Time alone is valuable not only for the child; it can also help a teacher focus on the child's positive attributes.

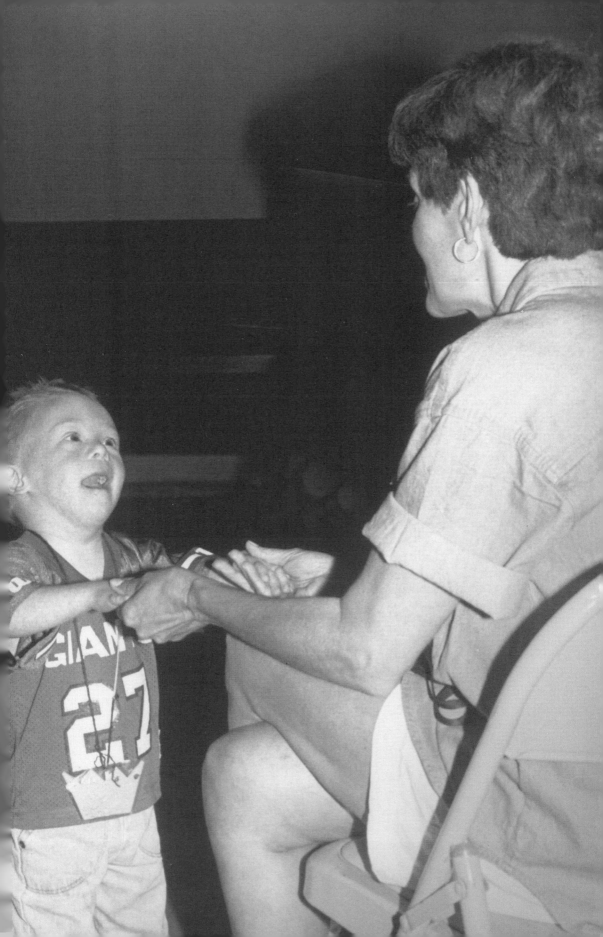

Postscript

Throughout this book we have tried to encourage teachers to observe and consider deeply the individual social dynamics children exhibit in early childhood settings. In addition, we have suggested reflection on the overall social structure of the classroom and the programs that provide the framework for social interactions within it.

People spend most of their lives in the company of others. The foundations of the capacity to function effectively in social contexts are laid during the first five or six years of life. Evidence suggests that the best time to help children with this major developmental challenge is during that same period. When young children begin to spend a large proportion of their time in group settings, adults have a unique opportunity to contribute to the processes of building a solid foundation for the children's social learning.

We suggest that social development be included in the assessments (formal and informal) of individual children's growth and learning throughout the early years. For this reason we have included an appendix that frames an approach to assessing social competence.

We also suggest that evaluations of the effectiveness and appropriateness of early childhood programs include observations of the extent to which opportunities for social interaction are available and teaching strategies relevant to social competence are applied. Evaluations should also address the impact of the curriculum approaches and materials used in children's social development.

One of the main themes for us throughout this discussion is the importance of teachers speaking to children—even young ones—as people with minds. We urge teachers to use warm, direct, matter-of-fact, and straightforward communication with children. It is unnecessary to be sentimental at one extreme or grim and somber at the other. We realize that everything we have suggested can be overdone, and that sometimes one suggestion may seem to contradict another. But there are no simple, easily applied formulas that solve the complexities involved in teaching young children. Nevertheless, we are persuaded by the evidence, our experiences, and the experiences of many colleagues that the early years are a propitious time to help children with achievement of social competence in the first of the four Rs—relationships.

Appendix

Assessing Children's Social Competence

In the preceding chapters we have presented our case for the preschool and early school years constituting the critical period for developing social competence; children's failure to do so may have lifelong consequences. It is therefore appropriate for teachers to assess children's social competence throughout this period.

We get frequent requests from teachers seeking help in assessing young children's progress toward social competence and in determining the potential seriousness of a child's social difficulties. In response to these requests, we have outlined a set of key attributes and social skills developed during the preschool and early school years (see page 106). Our intent is not to provide a prescription for "correct social behavior" but rather to help teachers to observe and document children's social development. Teachers can share this information with parents and use it as a basis for planning ways to support the child's social development.

When observing a child keep in mind that age is an important factor in deciding whether or not her social behavior warrants further examination. Some social competencies are just

emerging at age three; they may be tentative at age 4 and firmly established by age 6 or 7. Furthermore, temperament can account for substantial individual variation related to patterns of social behavior. For example, as we suggested in Chapter 1, some children are more shy by nature than are others. Keep in mind also that cultures and subcultures vary in what is considered acceptable and skilled behavior.

Finally, remember that, like adults, all children have some "off" days. Childhood is, by definition, a time for learning and testing many ways of responding to social situations. For informal assessments to be reasonably reliable, judgments of the child's *overall* pattern of functioning over a period of about a month are required.

When to seek outside help

As we stated earlier in the book, the least obtrusive approach to assessing a child's social competence is observation and monitoring of her behavior in the normal course of classroom activity. However, not all social difficulties can be addressed or alleviated in the classroom. We suggest that observation using a list of this kind can often support a teacher's suspicion that the child's social difficulties warrant further observation and follow-up intervention by a specialist—perhaps a school counselor, psychologist, or social worker. Some questions teachers (or parents, principals, or school counselors) might ask include the following:

1. Does the child exhibit problems in a number of the areas identified in the list?

2. Is there a long-standing pattern of difficulties—particularly aggressive behavior? Do the incidents of aggression seem to be increasing?

3. Are the social and behavioral problems of concern occurring in more than one of the child's social contexts? For example, are there reports of the child having social difficulties outside the classroom, at home, in the neighborhood, or in more than one classroom?

4. Do the behavior patterns of concern persist despite the assistance of the parents and teacher?

5. Is the behavior in question having a serious impact on other children? On the teacher? On the classroom atmosphere?

6. Does the child's behavior jeopardize the safety or rights of other children in the class?

If the teacher answers "yes" to one or more of these questions, or if her daily experiences with a child leads her to consider enlisting outside help, we recommend that she do so. The teacher can invite another teacher or the school counselor, for example, into the classroom to observe the incidents of concern and to suggest appropriate strategies for intervention. We encourage teachers to discuss the incidents and behavior with others and to involve the parents in every step taken.

The decision to seek assistance is rarely an easy one, and the remedies themselves can also be difficult. Parents are often upset, confused, and sometimes angry with the teacher and the school. Teachers can feel overwhelmed as well as frustrated and angry. Nevertheless, professional responsibility includes taking the next step—obtaining the help that can make a difference in the child's future. As one teacher put it,

> I have a child in my classroom this year about whom other teachers had warned me. After watching him with other children and seeing him in the classroom, I really dreaded dealing with him for an entire year! Although his parents were against it at first, we had him tested. Now a resource person comes into my classroom several times a week to assist me with strategies to help him. And by taking a little time each day to talk to him personally, I've really come to know a side of him that I wouldn't have known otherwise. You know, in many ways he's a sweet little boy. He's really trying now to get along in class and his social skills in particular are getting better.

Observing Children's Social Competence

Individual attributes

The child

1. is *usually* in a positive mood
2. is not *excessively* dependent on the teacher
3. *usually* comes to the program or setting willingly
4. *usually* copes with rebuffs and reverses adequately
5. shows the capacity to empathize with others
6. has positive relationships with one or two peers; shows the capacity to really care about them, miss them if they're absent, and so forth
7. displays the capacity for humor
8. does not seem to be acutely or chronically lonely

Social skills

The child usually

1. approaches others positively
2. expresses wishes and preferences clearly and gives reasons for her actions and positions
3. asserts his own rights and needs appropriately
4. is not easily intimidated by bullies
5. expresses frustration and anger effectively and without harming others, herself, or property
6. gains access to ongoing groups at play and work
7. enters ongoing discussions and makes relevant contributions to ongoing activities
8. takes turns fairly easily
9. shows interest in others; exchanges information with and requests information from others appropriately
10. negotiates and compromises with others appropriately
11. does not draw inappropriate attention to himself or disrupt the play or work of others
12. accepts and enjoys peers and adults of ethnic groups other than her own
13. interacts nonverbally with other children using smiles, waves, nods, and other appropriate gestures

Peer relationships

The child is

1. *usually* accepted rather than neglected or rejected by other children
2. *sometimes* invited by other children to join them in play, friendship, and work

References

Adams, J. 1953. Achievement and social adjustment of pupils in combination classes enrolling pupils of more than one grade level. *Journal of Educational Research* 47: 151–55.

Asher, S.R., S. Hymel, & P.D. Renshaw. 1984. Loneliness in children. *Child Development* 55: 1456–64.

Asher, S.R., & V.A. Wheeler. 1985. Children's loneliness: A comparison of rejected and neglected peer status. *Journal of Consulting and Clinical Psychology* 53: 500–05.

Barnett, W.S. 1997. *Lives in the balance: Age 27 benefit-cost analysis of the High/Scope Perry Preschool Program.* Ypsilanti, MI: High/Scope Press.

Baumrind, D. 1967. *Child care practices anteceding three patterns of preschool behavior.* Genetic Psychology Monographs, vol. 75, 43–88. Washington, DC: Heldref.

Baumrind, D. 1973. The development of instrumental competence through socialization. In *Minnesota Symposium on Child Psychology*, vol. 7, ed. A.D. Pick. Minneapolis: University of Minnesota Press.

Berk, L.E. 1994. Vygotsky's theory: The importance of make-believe play. *Young Children* 50 (1): 30–39.

Berk, L.E., & A. Winsler. 1995. *Scaffolding children's learning: Vygotsky and early childhood education.* Washington, DC: NAEYC.

Bierman, K.L., & W. Furman. 1984. Effects of social skills training and peer involvement on the social adjustment of preadolescents. *Child Development* 55: 151–62.

Boss, L. 1996. Personal communication.

Bronfenbrenner, U. 1970. *Two worlds of childhood: U.S. and U.S.S.R.* New York: Pocket Books.

Bronfenbrenner, U. 1986. Alienation and the four worlds of childhood. *Phi Delta Kappan* 67 (6): 430–36.

Bronfenbrenner, U. 1990. Who cares for children? *Research and Clinical Center for Child Development* 12: 27–40.

Brown, A., & A. Palincsar. 1989. Guided, cooperative learning and individual knowledge acquisition. In *Knowing, learning, and instruction: Essays in honor of Robert Glaser*, ed. L. Resnick. Hillsdale, NJ: Erlbaum.

Bruner, J. 1986. Play, thought, and language. *Prospects* 16 (1): 77–83.

Caine, R., & G. Caine. 1994. *Making connections: Teaching and the human brain.* Alexandria, VA: Association for Supervision and Curriculum Development.

Cairns, R.B. 1986. Contemporary perspectives on social development. In *Children's social behavior*, eds. P. Strain, M. Guralnick, & H. Walker. Orlando, FL: Academic.

Calkins, S.D. 1994. Origins and outcomes of individual differences in emotion regulation. In *The development of emotion regulation: Biological and behavioral considerations*, ed. N.A. Fox, 53–72. Monographs of the Society for Research in Child Developement, vol. 59, nos. 2–3, serial no. 240. Chicago: University of Chicago Press.

Cartledge, G., & J. Fellows-Milburn. 1980. *Teaching social skills to children.* New York: Pergamon.

Cassidy, J., & S.R. Asher. 1992. Loneliness and peer relations in young children. *Child Development* 63: 350–65.

Chao, R.K. 1994. Beyond parental control and authoritarian parenting styles: Understanding Chinese parenting through the cultural notion of training. *Child Development* 65: 1111–19.

Clarke–Stewart, A., C.P. Gruber, & L.M. Fitzgerald. 1994. *Children at home and in day care.* Hillsdale, NJ: Erlbaum.

Cochran, M., & V. Davila. 1992. Societal influences on children's peer relationships. In *Family-peer relationships*, eds. R.D. Parke & G.W. Ladd. Hillsdale, NJ: Erlbaum.

Coie, J.D., & K.A. Dodge. 1983. Continuities and changes in children's social status: A five-year longitudinal study. *Merrill-Palmer Quarterly* 29: 261–82.

Coie, J.D., & G. Krehbiel. 1984. Effects of academic tutoring on the social status of low-achieving, socially rejected children. *Child Development* 55: 1465–78.

Cole, P.M., M. Michel, & L. O'Donnell Teti. 1994. In *The development of emotion regulation and dysregulation: A clinical perspective*, ed. N.A. Fox, 73–100. Monographs of the Society for Research in Child Development, vol. 59, nos. 2–3, serial no. 240. Chicago: University of Chicago Press.

Coleman, J.S. 1987. The family and the schools. *Educational Researcher* 16 (60): 32–38.

Coleman, J. 1990. How worksite schools and other school reform can generate social capital (Editor's interview with James Coleman). *American Educator* (Summer): 35–45.

Connolly, J.A., & A. Doyle. 1983. Relation of social fantasy play to social competence in preschoolers. *Developmental Psychology* 20 (5): 797–806.

Cooney, J. 1996. Personal communication at Governors State University, University Park, Illinois.

Corsaro, W. 1985. *Friendship and peer culture in the early years*. Norwood, NJ: Ablex.

Cowen, E., A. Pederson, H. Babigian, L. Izzo, & M. Trost. 1973. Longterm follow-up of early detected vulnerable children. *Journal of Consulting and Clinical Psychology* 20 (5): 797–806.

Crockenberg, S., & C. Litman. 1990. Autonomy as competence in 2-year-olds: Maternal correlates of child defiance, compliance, and self-assertion. *Developmental Psychology* 26 (6): 961–71.

Csikszentmihalyi, M. 1990. *Flow: The psychology of optimal experience*. New York: Harper Perennial.

Delpit, L. 1988. The silenced dialogue: Power and pedagogy in educating other people's children. *Harvard Educational Review* 58 (3): 280–98.

Denham, S.A., S. Renwick-Debardi, & S. Hewes. 1994. Emotional communication between mothers and preschoolers: Relations with emotional competence. *Merrill-Palmer Quarterly* 40 (4): 488–89.

Denham, S.A., D. Zoller, & E.A. Couchoud. 1994. Socialization of preschoolers' emotion understanding. *Developmental Psychology* 30 (6): 928–36.

Derman-Sparks, L., & the A.B.C. Task Force. 1989. *Anti-bias curriculum: Tools for empowering young children*. Washington, DC: NAEYC.

Dewey, J. 1938. *Experience and education*. New York: Macmillan.

Dishion, T.J., G.R. Patterson, M. Stoolmiller, & M.L. Skinner. 1991. Family, school, and behavioral antecedents to early adolescent involvement with antisocial peers. *Developmental Psychology* 27 (1): 172–80.

Dodge, K.A. 1983. Behavioral antecedents of peer social status. *Child Development* 54: 1386–99.

Dodge, K.A., & J.D. Coie. 1989. Bully-victim relationships in boys' play groups. Paper presented at the Biennial Conference of the Society for Research in Child Development, Kansas City, Missouri.

Dumas, J.E., & P.J. LaFreniere. 1993. Mother–child relationships as sources of support or stress: A comparison of competent, average, aggressive and anxious dyads. *Child Development* 64: 1732–54.

Dunn, J. 1988. *The beginnings of social understanding*. Cambridge, MA: Harvard University Press.

Dweck, C.S., & E.S. Elliott. 1983. Achievement motivation. In *Handbook of child psychology, Vol. 4: Socialization, personality, and social development*. 4th ed., series ed. P.H. Mussen, vol. ed. E.M. Hetherington, 643–91. New York: Wiley.

Ekholm, B., & A. Hedin. 1985. Studies of day care center climate and its effect on children. Paper presented at the Symposium on Care, Rearing, and Education, Farohus, Sweden.

Ervin-Tripp, S. 1989. In *Sibling interactions across cultures: Theoretical and methodological issues*, ed. P.G. Zukow. New York: Springer–Verlag.

Feldman, S.S., & K.R. Wentzel. 1990. Relations among family interaction patterns, classroom self-restraint, and academic achievement in preadolescent boys. *Journal of Educational Psychology* 82 (4): 813–19.

Fox, N.A. 1989. Psychophysiological correlates of emotional reactivity during the first year of life. *Developmental Psychology* 25: 364–72.

Fox, N.A. 1994. Introduction to Part I. In *The development of emotion regulation: Biological and behavioral considerations*, ed. N.A. Fox, 3–6. Monographs of the Society for Research in Child Development, vol. 59, nos. 2–3, serial no. 240. Chicago: University of Chicago Press.

Freud, A., & S. Dann. 1951. An experiment in group upbringing. In *Psychoanalytic study of the child*, vol. 6, eds. R. Eisler et al. New York: International University Press.

Furman, W., D. Rahe, & W. Hartup. 1979. Rehabilitation of socially withdrawn preschool children through mixed-age and same-age socialization. *Child Development* 50: 915–22.

Gardner, H. 1991. *The unschooled mind: How children think and how schools should teach*. New York: Basic.

Goldman, J. 1981. A social participation of preschool children in same- versus mixed–age groups. *Child Development* 52: 644–50.

Goleman, D. 1995. *Emotional intelligence*. New York: Bantam.

Goodlad, J.I., & R.H. Anderson. 1987. *The non-graded elementary school*. New York: Teachers College Press.

Gottman, J.M. 1977. Toward a definition of social isolation in children. *Child Development* 48: 513–17.

Gottman, J.M. 1983. *How children become friends*. Monographs of the Society for Research in Child Development, vol. 48, no. 3, serial no. 291. Chicago: University of Chicago Press.

Gottman, J.M., & P. Schuler. 1976. Teaching social skills to isolated children. *Journal of Abnormal Child Psychology* 4: 179–97.

Gresham, F.M., & R.J. Nagle. 1984. Social skills training with children: Responsiveness to modeling and coaching as a function of peer orientation. *Journal of Consulting and Clinical Psychology* 48 (6): 718–29.

Halpern, R. 1990. Poverty and early childhood parenting: Toward a framework for intervention. *American Journal of Orthopsychiatry* 60 (1): 6–18.

Hartup, W. 1983. Peer relations. In *Handbook of child psychology, Vol. 4: Socialization, personality, and social development*. 4th ed., series ed. P.H. Mussen, vol. ed. E.M. Hetherington, 103–96. New York: Wiley.

Hartup, W. 1991. Having friends, making friends, and keeping friends: Relationships as educational contexts. In *Early report*. Minneapolis, MN: Center for Early Education and Development.

Hartup, W.W., & S.G. Moore. 1990. Early peer relations: Developmental significance and prognostic implications. *Early Childhood Research Quarterly* 5 (1): 1–18.

Haskins, R. 1985. Public school aggression among children with varying day-care experience. *Child Development* 56 (3): 689–703.

Hawkins, F.P. 1986. *The logic of action: Young children at work*. Boulder, CO: Association University Press.

Hazen, N., B. Black, & F. Fleming-Johnson. 1982. *Social acceptance: How children achieve it and how teachers can help*. Austin: University of Texas at Austin. ERIC, ED 241139.

Healy, J.M. 1990. *Endangered minds*. New York: Simon & Schuster.

Hetherington, E.M., vol. ed. 1983. *Vol. 4: Socialization, personality, and social development*. In *Handbook of child psychology*, 4th ed., series ed. P.H. Mussen. New York: Wiley.

Hewlett, S.A. 1986. *A lesser life: The myth of women's liberation in America*. New York: William Morrow.

Homel, R., A. Burns, & J. Goodnow. 1987. Parental social networks and child development. *Journal of Social and Personal Relationships* 4: 159–77.

Hubbard, J.A., & J.D. Coie. 1994. Emotional correlates of social competence in children's peer relationships. *Merrill-Palmer Quarterly* 40 (1): 1–20.

Hudley, C., & S. Graham. 1993. An attributional intervention to reduce peer-directed aggression among African American boys. *Child Development* 64 (1): 124–38.

Huges, F.P. 1995. *Children, play, and development*. Boston: Allyn & Bacon.

Hyden, L.C., B. Tarulli, & S. Hymel. 1988. Children talk about loneliness. Paper presented at the University of Waterloo Conference on Child Development, Waterloo, Canada.

Hymel, S., & S.R. Asher. 1977. *Assessment and training of isolated children's social skills*. Bethesda, MD: National Institute of Child Health and Human Development, National Institutes of Health. (BBB00456)

Hymel, S., K.H. Rubin, L. Rowden, & L. LeMare. 1990. Children's peer relationships: Longitudinal prediction of internalizing and externalizing problems from middle to late childhood. *Child Development* 61: 2004–21.

Johnson, C. 1986. My best friend hates me ... and other concerns of childhood. Paper presented at the Association for Childhood Education International Study Conference, Greensboro, North Carolina.

Johnson, D. 1991. *Learning together and alone: Cooperative, competitive, and individualistic learning*. Englewood Cliffs: NJ: Prentice Hall.

Johnson, D., R. Johnson, E. Johnson-Holubee, & P. Roy. 1984. *Circles of learning: Cooperation in the classroom*. Alexandria, VA: Association for Supervision and Curriculum Development.

Kagan, J. 1994. *The nature of emotion*. Monographs of the Society for Research in Child Development, vol. 59, nos. 2–3, serial no. 240. Chicago: University of Chicago Press.

Kamii, C. 1973. A sketch of the Piaget-derived preschool program. In *Revisiting early childhood education*, ed. J.L. Frost, 150–66. New York: Holt, Rinehart, & Winston.

Katz, L.G. 1990. Impressions of Reggio Emilia preschools. *Young Children* 45 (6): 4–10.

Katz, L. 1993. What can we learn from Reggio Emilia? In *The hundred languages of children: The Reggio Emilia approach to early childhood education*, eds. C. Edwards, L. Gandini, & G. Forman, 19–37. Norwood, NJ: Ablex.

Katz, L.G. 1995. *Talks with teachers of young children: A collection*. Norwood, NJ: Ablex.

Katz, L.G., & S.C. Chard. 1989. *Engaging children's minds: The project approach*. Norwood, NJ: Ablex.

Katz, L.G., D. Evangelou, & J.A. Hartman. 1990. *The case for mixed-age grouping in early education*. Washington, DC: NAEYC.

Kupersmidt, J. 1983. Predicting delinquency and academic problems from childhood peer status. Paper presented at the biennial meeting of the Society for Research in Child Development, Detroit, Michigan, 21–24 April.

Ladd, G.W. 1983. Social networks of popular, average, and rejected children in school settings. *Merrill-Palmer Quarterly* 29: 283–308.

LaGreca, A.M., & D.A. Santogrossi. 1984. Social skills training with elementary school students: A behavioral group approach. *Journal of Consulting and Clinical Psychology* 48: 220–27.

Lamb, M. 1978. The development of sibling relations in infancy: A short-term longitudinal study. *Child Development* 49: 1189–96.

Lane, H. 1947. Moratorium on grade grouping. *Educational Leadership* 4: 385–95.

Leavitt, R.L., & M.B. Power. 1989. Emotional socialization in the postmodern era: Children in day care. *Social Psychology Quarterly* 52 (1): 35–43.

Leight, R.L., & A.D. Rinehart. 1992. Revisiting Americana: One-room school in retrospect. *The Educational Forum* 56 (2): 133–51.

Lewis, C.C. 1995. *Educating hearts and minds: Reflections on Japanese preschool and elementary education*. New York: Cambridge University Press.

Maccoby, E.E. 1980. *Social development*. New York: Harcourt Brace Jovanovich.

Madsen, C.H., Jr., W.C. Becker, & D.R. Thomas. 1968. Rules, praise, and ignoring: Elements of elementary classroom control. *Journal of Applied Behavior Analysis* 1: 139–50.

McClellan, D.E. 1989. Social skill training intervention with aggressive young children. Urbana, IL. ERIC, ED 312035.

McClellan, D.E. 1994. Research on multiage grouping: Implications for education. In *Full circle: Reinventing multiage education*, eds. P. Chase & J. Dohn. Portsmouth, NH: Heinemann.

McClellan, D.E., & S. Kinsey. 1997. Children's social behavior in relationship to participation in mixed-age or same-age classrooms. Paper presented at the biennial meeting of the Society for Research in Child Development, Washington, D.C., 3–6 April.

Meier, D. 1991. The kindergarten tradition in high school. In *Progressive education for the 1990s: Transforming practice*, eds. K. Jervis & C. Montag. New York: Schocken.

Michael, C.M., D.P. Morris, & E. Soroker. 1957. Follow-up studies of shy, withdrawn children II: Relative incidence of schizophrenia. *American Journal of Orthopsychiatry* 27: 1331–37.

Miller, S.A. 1995. Parents' attributions for their children's behavior. *Child Development* 66: 1557–84.

Mize, J., & G.W. Ladd. 1990. Toward the development of successful social skills training for preschool children. In *Peer rejection in childhood*, eds. S.R. Asher & J.D. Coie, 338–61. New York: Cambridge University Press.

Montessori, M. 1964. *The Montessori method*. New York: Schocken.

Moorhouse, E. 1971. The philosophy underlying the British primary school. In *Teaching in the British primary school*, ed. V.R. Rogers. London: Macmillan.

Morris, D.P., E. Soroker, & G. Burruss. 1954. Follow-up studies of shy, withdrawn children: Evaluation of later adjustment. *American Journal of Orthopsychiatry* 24: 743–55.

O'Conner, R.D. 1969. Modification of social withdrawal through symbolic modeling. *Journal of Applied Behavior Analysis* 2: 15–22.

O'Conner, R.D. 1972. Relative efficiency of modeling, shaping, and the combined procedures for modification of social withdrawal. *Abnormal Psychology* 79: 327–34.

Oden, S., & S.R. Asher. 1977. Coaching children in skills for friendship-making. *Child Development* 48 (2): 495–507.

Oden, S., & P.R. Ramsey. 1993. Implementing research on children's social competence: What do teachers and researchers need to learn? *Exceptionality Education Canada* 3 (1 & 2): 209–32.

Olds, A., & R. Olds, Associates. 1989. Psychological and physiological harmony in child care center design. *Children's Environments Quarterly* 6 (4): 8–16.

Packer, M.J., & E. Richardson. 1989. Strategies of social entry among preschool children. Paper presented at the biennial conference of the Society for Research in Child Development, Kansas City, Missouri.

Paley, V. 1992. *You can't say you can't play*. Cambridge, MA: Harvard University Press.

Palmer, P.J. 1987. Community, conflict, and ways of knowing: Ways to deepen our educational agenda. *Change* (September/October): 20–25.

Parke, R.D., & R.G. Slaby. 1983. The development of aggression. In *Handbook of child psychology, Vol. 4: Socialization, personality, and social development*. 4th ed., series ed. P.H. Mussen, vol. ed. E.M. Hetheringon, 547–641. New York: Wiley.

Parker, J.G., & S.R. Asher. 1987. Peer relations and later personal adjustment: Are low-accepted children at risk? *Psychological Bulletin* 102: 357–89.

Parpal, M., & E.E. Maccoby. 1985. Maternal responsiveness and subsequent child compliance. *Child Development* 56 (5): 1236–34.

Paul, J.J., & R. Simeonsson. 1993. *Children with special needs: Family, culture and society.* New York: Harcourt Brace Javonovich.

Pellegrini, A.D., & C.D. Glickman. 1990. Measuring kindergartners' social competence. *Young Children* 45 (4): 40–44.

Peplau, L.A., & D. Perlman. 1982. *Loneliness: A sourcebook of current theory, research and therapy.* New York: Wiley.

Piaget, J. 1970. *Structuralism.* Edited and translated by C. Machler. New York: Basic.

Power, M.B. 1985. The ritualization of emotional conduct in childhood. In *Studies in symbolic interaction,* vol. 6, ed. N.K. Denzin. Greenwich, CT: JAI Press.

Pratt, D. 1983. Age segregation in schools. Paper presented at the annual meeting of the American Educational Research Association, Montreal, Quebec, Canada, April.

Prawat, R.S., & J.R. Nickerson. 1985. The relationship between teacher thought and action and student affective outcomes. *The Elementary School Journal* 85: 529–40.

Prescott, E., & E. Jones. 1985. *Environments for young children.* South Carolina Educational Television Network. Washington, DC: NAEYC. Videotape.

Putallaz, M., & J.M. Gottman. 1981. An interactional model of children's entry into peer groups. *Child Development* 52 (3): 986–94.

Rabiner, D., & J. Coie. 1989. Effect of expectancy inductions on rejected children's acceptance by unfamiliar peers. *Developmental Psychology* 25 (3): 450–57.

Ratner, H., & L. Stettner. 1991. Thinking and feeling: Putting Humpty Dumpty together again. *Merrill-Palmer Quarterly* 37 (1): 1–26.

Ratzki, A. 1988. Creating a school community: One model of how it can be done. *American Educator* (Spring): 10–42.

Rivkin, M.S. 1995. *The great outdoors: Restoring children's right to play outside.* Washington, DC: NAEYC.

Robins, L.N. 1974. *Deviant children grow up.* Huntington, NY: Robert E. Krieger.

Rogoff, B.M. 1990. *Apprenticeship in thinking: Cognitive development in social context.* New York: Oxford University Press.

Rogoff, B.M. 1997. *Development as transformation of participation in sociocultural activities.* Presentation at the biennial meeting of the Society for Research in Child Development, Washington, D.C., 3–5 April.

Rogoff, B., J. Mistry, A. Goncu, C. Mosier. 1993. *Guided participation in cultural activity by toddlers and caregivers.* Monographs of the Society for Research in Child Development, vol.

58, no. 8, serial no. 236. Chicago: University of Chicago Press.

Ross, H., C. Tesla, B. Kenyon, & S. Lollis. 1990. Maternal intervention in toddler peer conflict: The socialization of principles of justice. *Developmental Psychology* 26 (6): 994–1003.

Rubin, K., & B. Everett. 1982. Social perspective-taking in young children. In *The young child: Reviews of research,* vol. 3, eds. S.G. Moore & C.R. Cooper. Washington, DC: NAEYC.

Rubin, Z. 1983. The skills of friendship. In *Early childhood development and education,* eds M. Donaldson, R. Grieve, & C. Pratt. New York: Guilford.

Rudolph, K.D., C. Harmen, & D. Burge. 1995. Cognitive representations of self, family, and peers in school competence and sociometric status. *Child Development* 66 (5): 1385–1402.

Schwartz, D., K.A. Dodge, & J.D. Coie. 1993. The emergence of chronic peer victimization in boys' play groups. *Child Development* 64: 1755–72.

Schwarz, J.C. 1972. Effects of peer familiarity on the behavior of preschoolers in a novel situation. *Journal of Personality and Social Psychology* 24: 276–84.

Schweinhart, L., D. Weikart, & M. Larner. 1986. Consequences of three preschool curriculum models through age 15. *Early Childhood Research Quarterly* 1: 15–45.

Shure, M.B. 1992. *I can problem solve.* Champaign, IL: Research Press.

Slaby, R.G., W.C. Roedell, D. Arezzo, & K. Hendrix. 1995. *Early violence prevention: Tools for teachers of young children.* Washington, DC: NAEYC.

Smilansky, S., & L. Shefatya. 1990. *Facilitating play: A medium for promoting cognitive, socioemotional, and academic development in young children.* Gaithersburg, MD: Psychosocial & Educational Publications.

Steinberg, L., S.M. Dornbusch, & B. Brown. 1992. Ethnic differences in adolescent achievement: An ecological perspective. *American Psychologist* 47 (6): 723–29.

Stipek, D.J., J.H. Gralinski, & C.B. Kopp. 1990. Self-concept development in the toddler years. *Developmental Psychology* 26 (6): 972–97.

Suomi, S., & H. Harlow. 1975. The role and reason of peer relationships in Rhesus monkeys. In *Friendships and peer relations,* eds. M. Lewis & L. Rosenblum, 153–86. New York: Wiley.

Theilheimer, R. 1993. Something for everyone: Benefits of mixed-age grouping. *Young Children* 48 (5): 85–87.

Tobin, J.J., D.Y. Wu, & D.H. Davidson. 1989. *Preschool in three cultures.* New Haven, CT: Yale University Press.

Vandell, D.L., & S.E. Hembree. 1994. Peer social status and friendship: Independent contributors to children's social and academic adjustment. *Merrill-Palmer Quarterly* 40 (4): 461–77.

Veenman, S. 1995. Cognitive and noncognitive effects of multigrade and multi-age classes: A best-evidence synthesis. *Review of Educational Research* 65 (4): 319–81.

Vygotsky, L. 1978. *Mind, self, and society*. Chicago: University of Chicago Press.

Waters, E., & L.A. Sroufe. 1983. Social competence as a developmental construct. *Developmental Review* 3: 79–97.

Werner, J.S., & R.S. Smith. 1982. *Vunerable but invincible*. New York: McGraw-Hill.

Whiting, B., & J. Whiting. 1975. *Children of six cultures: A psycho-cultural analysis*. Cambridge, MA: Harvard University Press.

Wood, G. 1992. *Schools that work: America's most innovative public education programs*. New York: Dutton.

Zahavi, S., & S.R. Asher. 1978. The effect of verbal instruction on preschool children's aggressive behavior. *Journal of School Psychology* 16: 146–53.

Zahn-Waxler, C., S. Friedman, & M. Cummings. 1983. Children's emotions and behaviors in response to infants' cries. *Child Development* 54: 1522–28.

Zerby, J. 1961. A comparison of academic achievement and social adjustment of primary school children in the graded and ungraded school programs. Ph.D. diss., Pennsylvania State University.

Zimbardo, P.G. 1977. *Shyness*. Reading, MA: Addison-Wesley.